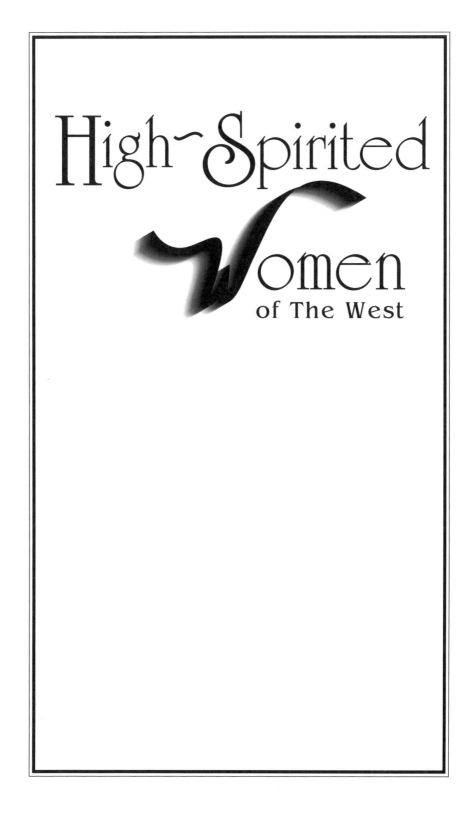

High~Spirited

Women

of The West

HIGH~SPIRITED WOMEN OF THE WEST
by Anne Seagraves ©1992

*Other non-fiction books
by Anne Seagraves*

Daughters of the West: © 1996

Soiled Doves: Prostitution in the Early West: © 1994

Women Who Charmed the West: © 1991

Women of the Sierra: © 1990

Tahoe Lake In The Sky: © 1987

Beautiful Lake County: © 1985

◆――――――――――――――――――――――――――――◆

High~Spirited Women of The West

By Anne Seagraves

Published by WESANNE PUBLICATIONS
Post Office Box 428
Hayden, Idaho 83835

Library of Congress Number 92-90926
ISBN 0-9619088-3-1

Arizona Historical Society, Tucson, AZ; Arizona, University of, Tucson, AZ; Bancroft Library, Berkeley, CA; British Columbia Archives and Records, Victoria, B.C.; California History Center Foundation, De Anza College, Cupertino, CA; California Historical Society, San Francisco, CA; California State Library, Sacramento, CA; California, University of, Berkeley, CA; Denver Public Library, Denver, CO; Grace Hudson Museum and Sun House, Ukiah, CA; Lane County Historical Museum, Eugene, OR; Lake County Library, Lakeport, CA; Mariposa Historical Society, Mariposa, CA; Nevada Historical Society, Las Vegas, NV; Nevada Historical Society, Reno, NV; Nevada State Library, Carson City, NV; Nevada, University of, Las Vegas, NV; Nevada, University of, Reno, NV; Oklahoma Historical Society, Oklahoma City, OK; Oklahoma, University of, Norman, OK; Oregon Historical Society, Portland, OR; Oregon, University of, Eugene, OR; Society of California Pioneers, San Francisco, CA; Utah Historical Society, Salt Lake City, UT; Utah, University of, Salt Lake City, UT; and The Women's Heritage Museum, Palo Alto, CA.

During the research for *High-Spirited Women of the West*, many individuals were extremely helpful. The author would like to express her appreciation to the following people:

The staff of the California State Library; Peter Bandurraga, Ph.D., Director of the Nevada Historical Society, Reno, NV; Dot Brovarney, Curator, and Suzanne Abel-Vidor, Director, Grace Hudson Museum and Sun House, Ukiah, CA; Jack Fiske, Tombstone, AZ; Ben T. Traywick, Tombstone, AZ, for the special photo of Nellie Cashman; and Bobbie Schiavelli, Simi Valley, CA.

AND A VERY SPECIAL THANK YOU TO:
Marge Boynton, The Sun House Guild, Ukiah, CA., for letting me use her late husband's book, *The Painter Lady, Grace Carpenter Hudson*; Barbara Bush, Arizona Historical Society, Tuscon, AZ., material for the Nellie Cashman story; Lee Mortensen, Librarian, Nevada Historical Society, Reno, NV, for always being there with the right answer; and Carrie Townley-Porter for making the Helen Jane Stewart story possible.

Through the ages women have had to reconcile themselves to being placed beneath men, both socially and politically. Because the average women of the 19th century had neither the education nor the experience to broaden their lives, many were forced to live a sterile, unproductive existence. Some however, consistently refused to accept the role of a second-rate citizen. Those women have struggled during the last few centuries to gain their independence.

During the 1800s, women were dependent upon the family, with little or no opportunity to function as individuals. Their only social contacts were within their churches, and they seldom ventured outside their own households. Men, on the other hand, gathered in taverns, at town meetings, and at social clubs. They were the dominant rulers of their wives and children. Women took subordinate roles, remaining invisible in public life.

By 1830 a small number of women began to move beyond the home to work in factories or as domestics. They usually labored an average of 12 hours a day, six days a week under unhealthy working conditions for little pay. With the advent of the Civil War, more opportunities became available, but women continued to be treated as inferior. The average female wage earner was usually young, single, unskilled, and lived in an urban area. She was most likely to be the illiterate daughter of an immigrant and did not expect to remain in the employment market because she planned to marry.

Because women accepted lower wages, they were welcomed into the work force. A woman would perform a man's duties for less pay, without chance for advancement. She had been taught that she was of no value, and she had low self-esteem with little hope of receiving an education. Working women also suffered from a society that believed a woman's place was in the home. They were pulled in all directions.

Within the churches women were expected to be pious and pure and to stay in their proper place. They were told to remain passionless and devoid of any sexual desires, as the only superiority they had over men was their moral values. The medical profession also confirmed that a lack of passion was a commendable trait. Doctors wrote long papers recommending restraint to assure a healthy body. They further stressed that women were mentally and physically inferior to men.

During that era, it seemed no matter what a woman did she was morally or socially wrong. If she followed her minister's or her doctor's advice, her husband would force her to submit to his desires or seek to fulfill them elsewhere. If she complied, having no means of birth control, she would probably bear eight to 12 children. In general married women were at the mercy of their husbands, while the unmarried women lived faded lives, and became burdens to their relatives or society.

Although a young woman usually chose her mate, once she married she had neither choice of where to live nor control over the property she brought with her to the marriage. Both the wife and her property belonged to her husband, and he made all the decisions. When the wife bore children, she had no legal authority over them. She was only there to take care of their physical needs and those of her husband. Since women had never been given equal educational rights, they were unable to deal with business or understand politics, remaining helpless and weaker individuals with negative self-images. The only pride a woman had was in motherhood.

Despite all these obstacles, women managed to obtain upward mobility. In the mid-1800s, many became rebellious feminists who pushed aside the mores of society. Some masqueraded as men, becoming loners. Others, confronted the problem head-on as women, defying society to stop them. Eventually women began to express their own desires and political viewpoints, first as individuals, then in groups. They had become rebels who wanted control over their own bodies and lives.

In 1869, the women of Wyoming were the first to exercise the right to vote, with the women of Utah and Colorado following. One by one the states and territories allowed suffrage, and in 1920 the 19th Amendment granted American women full voting privileges.

Although the women of today have the right to vote, their movement continues. Suffrage in the 19th century merely opened the door to equality in the 20th century; unfortunately, it did not guarantee it.

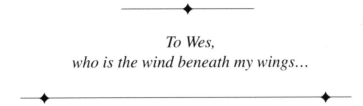

To Wes,
who is the wind beneath my wings...

CONTENTS

ACKNOWLEDGMENTS .... *vii*

FOREWORD .... *ix*

INTRODUCTION .... *xv*

CHAPTER:

1. JESSIE BENTON FRÉMONT, A Lifetime of Extremes 19

2. ABIGAIL SCOTT DUNIWAY,
   "The Grand Old Lady of Oregon" 41

3. SARAH WINNEMUCCA, The Sagebrush Princess 57

4. FANNY STENHOUSE AND ANN ELIZA YOUNG,
   The Tyranny of Polygamy 77

5. BELLE STARR, Petticoat Desperado 101

6. NELLIE CASHMAN, The Irish Angel of Mercy 123

7. JEANNE ELIZABETH WIER,
   Northern Nevada's Noted Historian 135

8. HELEN JANE WISER STEWART,
   The First Lady of Southern Nevada 143

9. GRACE CARPENTER HUDSON, A Lady With a Paint Brush 159

   BIBLIOGRAPHY 172

Cover Photo: Nellie Cashman
Courtesy of the Arizona Historical Society

This book about yesterday's women has been produced
by these women of today...
Anne Seagraves, Author/Publisher
Susan Stout, Editor
Julie A. Knudsen, Graphic Artist
Betsy R. Andrews, Proof Reader
Printed by, Janice Caravantes

This book profiles the lives of ten courageous women from the mid-1800s through the turn of the century. They were the high-spirited women of the West who left conventional roles behind, becoming America's early feminists.

Although there were many notable women in the 19th century, the women in this book were chosen for their diversity and unusual lifestyles. Some of these women are famous; those who aren't should be. Most of the ladies were well-educated offspring of leading families; a few were self-taught. Each set out to achieve her goal in a different area of the West during the same time period, yet only two of the women ever met.

These entertaining and inspiring stories bring to life the women who helped shape history. Each one was different — all made contributions to society.

The dashing Belle Starr, America's famous female desperado, and Nellie Cashman, a fun-loving, non-conforming lady prospector, were considered **bold**. While Belle rode across the Oklahoma Territory beside a band of ruthless bandits, the petite Nellie was prospecting for gold in areas from Alaska to Nevada.

Sarah Winnemucca, the Paiute Princess, and Abigail Duniway, an Oregon suffragette, were **dedicated** to their causes. Sarah spent her lifetime traveling across the Northwest fighting for the rights of her people, while Abigail waged a 42-year battle to secure the vote for the women of Oregon. Others — like Jessie Fremont, a woman who bore her triumphs without arrogance and her defeats without bitterness — were dedicated to the people they loved.

Utah's Fanny Stenhouse and Ann Eliza Young were caught in the bitter web of polygamy. Fanny chose to patiently wait for her freedom, but the **rebellious** Ann Eliza began a battle that helped to end multiple marriage.

In Nevada, the quiet Helen Stewart, a widow with five children, managed a 2,000-acre ranch and founded Las Vegas. Grace Hudson, an artist from California, preserved the history and rich heritage of the Pomo Indians, and pages from historian Jeanne Wier's diary reveal her difficult and sometimes humorous travels through early Nevada.

From suffragette to lady rancher to female desperado, they set the groundwork for the liberties modern women often take for granted. This book tells of the strong, high-spirited women of the West and the people they touched as they dared to blaze new trails for the women of the 20th century.

The stories of these remarkable women have been carefully researched and documented through the generous assistance of historians, librarians and the special collection departments of many leading universities.

I have spent years reading old, out-of-print books, biographies, newspapers dating from the late 1800s to the mid-1900s, magazines, diaries, public records, and correspondence.

As with all history, one must rely upon what others have written or recorded. In this book, I have attempted to create readable, accurate stories of these noteworthy women of yesterday and their achievements.

— The Author

Jessie Benton Frémont

Chapter 1

JESSIE BENTON FRÉMONT
◆————————————————————————◆
A Lifetime of Extremes

J essie Benton Frémont lived a life of significant successes and painful failures. As "Our Jessie" she came close to the center of power during her husband's presidential campaign. Her consuming love for John C. Frémont, an illusive man who drifted in and out of her life always seeking new horizons, brought both happiness and despair. In her own words Jessie said, *"I am like a deep ship. I drive best under a strong wind,"* — an apt description for this fascinating woman who witnessed and influenced history.

Jessie Ann Benton was born at her mother's home near Lexington, Virginia, on May 31, 1824. She was the second daughter of Thomas Hart Benton, a noted senator from Missouri, and Elizabeth McDowell, a lovely Southern belle. The senator was a shrewd, self-made man who was filled with fiery ambition. His wife Elizabeth was a quiet, genteel woman. Although the couple had six children — four girls and two boys — it was Jessie who captured her father's heart with her robust health and vigorous personality. He named her after his father, Jesse; and Senator Benton and his daughter became early companions. It was a strong bond that, although sometimes was painful, lasted throughout Jessie's life.

As Jessie grew from a precocious little girl into her teens, she enjoyed a multicultural life. From her mother's side of the family she learned the elegant ways of the South. On every even year the Bentons would travel over the Blue Ridge Mountains, down into the peaceful valley that was part of Cherry Grove plantation. It was a large estate surrounded by rolling fields of tobacco that were worked by the McDowell family's slaves. Although the McDowells' way of life was a part of the slow, easy pace of the South, Thomas Benton was never comfortable with slavery. Years later, when

Elizabeth's father died, she freed the slaves she inherited.

To Jessie, the trip to Cherry Grove meant losing her independence. During the family's visit she would be requested to keep her hair neatly combed and to wear starched dresses and fancy shoes. She was usually considered a misfit at her mother's home. Everyone knew that during the visit, Jessie's boisterous behavior would eventually get her into trouble and she would be frowned upon by the refined McDowell family. While in Virginia, Jessie learned that Southern women were expected to know their place and remain there. It provided a lesson for the outspoken girl; and although she loved her McDowell grandparents, she was always glad when it was time to leave.

During the odd-numbered years the family went to the Senator's home in St. Louis, Missouri, where his mother lived with only her servants. She had lost her husband and several of her children to tuberculosis, and she spent the rest of her life in the large two-story house overlooking the main square. The elder Mrs. Benton was always happy to see her son and his family. It eased her loneliness.

While in Missouri, Thomas Benton took care of political affairs and talked of the new frontier. St. Louis was a wide-open community at the edge of the wilderness. The senator enjoyed listening to the tales of the French and Spanish fur traders who shared their adventures and the excitement of the West with him.

To Jessie, St. Louis was a vivid city filled with colorful people. It was an ambitious community bursting with life, and the eager little girl spent her time observing the different cultures. Along the streets she saw immigrants wearing wooden shoes, fur traders dressed in buckskins, and black-frocked missionaries. Her ears were filled with the lively music of the traveling minstrels and the sad songs of the Negro slaves as they loaded the steamers on the waterfront. St. Louis was a place to remember, and it was here that Jessie learned tolerance and acceptance of all people.

The Bentons' third home was in Washington, D.C., where the family lived during the winter when Congress was in session. Their home was a prestigious brick house with high ceilings and large, comfortable rooms often filled with laughing children. During Jessie's young years, the Capitol was a raw, sprawling city of strange faces and excitement. It contained a blend of elegantly attired statesmen, visiting diplomats, and poor families who lived in squalid shacks. There were also gala parties and afternoon teas. In Washington, women were granted more freedom. Many were seen in public without male escorts — something that would never be allowed in the South.

It was this rich, robust city that Jessie liked the best. Here, she would accompany her father to his office; she was as comfortable running around at the White House as she was at home. It was a natural thing to see the little tomboy sitting by Andrew Jackson's side as he ran his fingers through her curly hair. She knew all the leading lawmakers and was not afraid to speak out. The senator admired Jessie's spunk, and he encouraged her to be herself.

Thomas Benton was very much in control of his family. His wife Elizabeth was a semi-invalid, so he selected tutors for the children and spent many hours personally supervising their studies. He also took excellent care of their health. The specter of his family's lung problems was never far from his mind. Everyone wore sensible clothing and received fresh air and exercise. They ate well-balanced, nourishing meals. Despite his efforts, Thomas and Elizabeth lost two children to the dreaded tuberculosis.

When Jessie was 14 years old, her father decided she would attend Miss English's Academy in Georgetown. Jessie did not want to go, but the Senator was adamant as he wanted the best for his Jessie. This was the first time that Jessie and her father had seriously disagreed. Although the girl was proficient in academics and spoke French and Spanish fluently, he believed she needed to have a polished background. So she was packed off to the academy, protesting all the way! Needless to say, the high-spirited girl did not get along well with her teachers or her high-society classmates. Social position and wealth never impressed Jessie; her friends were a mixture of both the rich and not-so-rich. She never adapted to Miss English or the academy, and she was allowed to return home a year later, when she was 15 years old.

Jessie had blossomed into a lovely young woman. She possessed a classic oval face with dark, sassy eyes, rich reddish hair, and a slender build. Because her mother was ill a great deal of the time and her older sister was away from home, Jessie took over as hostess for her father's many dinner parties. She was an excellent conversationalist who could discuss any subject. During this period Jessie entertained several prominent people. It was at one of these affairs she met Lieutenant John C. Frémont, a handsome man 11 years her senior, with whom she immediately fell in love.

This was the beginning of a strong, enduring love that would last throughout their lifetimes. It was a mutual attraction, for John fell deeply in love with the vibrant Jessie. In his memoirs Frémont wrote, *"She was only 15, but the bloom of her girlish beauty captivated me. Her qualities were all womanly... There had been no experience of life to brush away the bloom. She had inherited from her father his grasp of mind, comprehending with a tenacious memory ..."* [1]

John Frémont was filled with the glamour of the West. He was born January 21, 1813, in Savannah, Georgia, the illegitimate son of a beautiful Southern woman and a French émigré, Jean Charles Fremon. While growing up John suffered the embarrassment of his birth. He was an ambitious young man who yearned for the security of a normal home.

At the age of 14, John was apprenticed as a clerk to a lawyer. When the youth proved to be extremely bright, the lawyer sent him to study under an Edinburgh scholar. John, who had changed his name to Frémont, was 16 when he went on to college where he excelled at math. Following college he became a math instructor, then a surveyor, and eventually obtained a commission with the United States Corps of Topographical Engineers. Shortly afterward he met Jean-Nicolas Nicollet, a French explorer who became an important figure in John's life. Together they successfully completed a government expedition to the Dakota Country, and Nicollet helped teach Frémont the art of preparing the materials they had collected. When Senator Benton met Frémont, the young man was 27 years old and had completed several Western expeditions.

The love between Jessie and John soon became obvious to her parents, who were not at all pleased with the turn of events. Although the senator admired Frémont for his adventurous spirit

1 **A Man Unafraid**, by Herbert Bashford and Harr Wagner

and knowledge of the West, he did not think John was the man for Jessie. She was too young for marriage; and Frémont, who had no family name or funds, faced an obscure future. Thomas Benton, however, knew his strong-willed daughter. He made the couple promise to wait one year, until Jessie was 17, before considering marriage.

Benton hoped Jessie's attraction for John was temporary, but nothing could keep the young lovers apart. John Frémont was a charismatic man who was 5 feet, 9 inches tall, with a sinewy, graceful build, brown curly hair and piercing blue eyes. He shared many traits with Jessie. They were both impulsive, high-spirited, nomadic people who loved adventure. To the pair, a year was too long; so when Frémont returned from his expedition, he and the 17-year-old Jessie eloped.

Following the wedding, Jessie returned home, planning to keep the marriage a secret. In Washington, however, where the Benton family was well-known, there could be no secrets. When Senator Benton found out, he was furious with his daughter and refused to condone her marriage. Jessie, who was just as strong as her father, left her home on the arm of her husband, and the Frémonts became the talk of Washington's high society.

John Frémont gained more than a wife when he married Jessie Benton. He had wed a woman who would stand by his side, lending him the strength and support he desperately needed. She brought with her a knowledge of politics and a cultured background which included the friendship of many important statesmen. They soon became the most sought after couple in Washington and were seen at all the important parties and dances. John, in his uniform of black and gold, and the radiant Jessie dressed in velvet and lace were a handsome pair.

Thomas and Elizabeth Benton carefully followed the progress of their daughter and her new husband, and a month after the marriage they invited them to return home. The offer was accepted, and the newlyweds packed their bags and moved to the Bentons' house. They settled down to live a lifetime of rare devotion and love. Within the warm, friendly atmosphere of Jessie's home, John Frémont found the security he had long been seeking.

An alliance was soon formed between Benton and Frémont, who shared a mutual desire for a series of expeditions that would provide a map to the West. Benton believed it was the duty of the United States to open the entire continent for Western migration. He also wanted to prevent the British from taking control of the rich territories of California and Oregon. As chairman of the committee which controlled the funds for the Topographical Bureau, Benton found a way to finance a trip. Nicollet was chosen to head the party, but due to his ill health and advancing age the job fell to John Frémont, who took full charge of the expedition. Although she hated to see her husband leave so soon after their marriage, Jessie was in complete agreement with the expedition. She fully shared their dreams of Western expansion and did not want to stand in the way of Frémont's future. Jessie was also an ambitious woman who was proud of her husband's accomplishments.

Time passed quickly as preparations for the expedition got under way. The young couple enjoyed every moment they shared, but both dreaded their imminent separation. They attended a whirlwind of social activities and spent three memorable months before it was time for Frémont to leave. When the last farewell arrived, Jessie helped her husband into his uniform and, although she was expecting a child and needed him close by, Jessie said good-bye with a smile. She wanted John to carry only happy memories.

Following his departure, loneliness set in for Jessie. She would pace restlessly around the house. She lost her sparkle, and shadows appeared beneath her young eyes. Senator Benton was concerned about his daughter's health as he knew how much she loved and missed her husband. He finally decided Jessie needed something to take her mind off Frémont, so he put her to work copying important papers. During the following weeks, father and daughter spent their days together in peaceful companionship. This quiet life was interrupted when her mother collapsed from a stroke and became partially paralyzed. The senator, who adored his gentle Elizabeth, became a helpless man: Jessie took over the responsibilities of the home, as well as nursing her sick mother.

Frémont returned in October, triumphant from his first trans-

Missouri expedition. He had successfully found a route over the Rockies and raised the Stars and Stripes upon the highest pinnacle—one that was almost a needle point. His homecoming was a joyful event that brought happiness back into the Bentons' life. He also arrived in time to share the birth of their first child, Elizabeth, who was named after Jessie's mother. She was a strong, healthy baby who soon acquired the nickname of "Lily."

Once home, Frémont had to document his official report, but he was unable to write. He had seen too many things, and the party had accomplished so much that the words wouldn't flow. Frémont wanted to share the splendor of the country and of the men who accompanied him, especially the noted scout, Kit Carson. Carson was returning from St. Louis when Frémont hired him as a guide. He had spent his life as a trapper and scout, was an unerring shot, a successful Indian fighter, and one of the most celebrated men in the annals of Western history. Frémont was impressed with this mountain man who possessed courage and a great honesty. He wanted to put it all on paper to share with the world.

Jessie at this point realized how she could help her husband. John could dictate his report and she would write it. Soon the husband and wife became collaborators. They spent hours reviewing John's notes. Using his scientific facts and vivid descriptions, Jessie provided the expertise to weave the reports into brilliant, readable literature. The expedition came alive on paper and created a sensation. The reports were seized upon by publishers, and some of the editions ran into the thousands. Words of praise for the daring explorer came from around the world. John Frémont became the man of the hour. While he was hailed as a national hero, Jessie stood quietly in the background. As a woman, she knew it was only through John that she would become famous.

As praise of the reports spread, Frémont was asked to lead another expedition. It was to be one of great importance. The government wanted a survey to the Pacific, and Senator Benton's ambition was to see the United States flag waving from coast to coast. Frémont received his appointment; and Jessie, although she hated to see him leave so soon, took a genuine interest in the plans. By then she was handling all of Frémont's correspondence.

In the spring of 1843 Frémont left Washington for St. Louis, traveling with his wife and Lily. Jessie planned to remain in St. Louis until her husband's return, which was expected to be about eight months later. Frémont requested a howitzer from the arsenal at St. Louis. He thought the gun would be effective in encounters with hostile Indians. The colonel in command, who was an old friend of the Bentons, approved the howitzer without official government documentation. The following day Frémont left for the frontier to prepare for the journey. Soon after his departure, Jessie opened a letter to her husband from the War Department demanding that he return immediately to Washington. The department wanted an explanation for the need of a howitzer on a scientific expedition. Jessie was only 18 years old, and her father was not with her to provide advice. Jessie knew that if John returned to Washington he would lose the valuable expedition to someone else. Time was critical. Without hesitation, Jessie sent a message to Frémont urging him to proceed immediately with the expedition. She told him, *"Make haste, do not ask why — only go."* When the messenger returned, John's words to Jessie were, *"I trust and GO."* When Senator Benton heard what Jessie had done, he stood by his daughter's decision.[1]

Jessie and Lily settled into her father's home in St. Louis to await Frémont's return. The few messages from John were spread out over the months. The holidays came, and Jessie and Lily decorated their first Christmas tree alone while John was freezing in Nevada. Jessie was worried and lonely. By January, she was ill with concern. In March she was frantic. April brought hope. In June there was news that Frémont had reached California following a terrible ordeal crossing the Sierra. John had been gone for more than a year, and Jessie missed him desperately. Late one night in August he returned. He was tired and thin — and Jessie welcomed her adventurer with open, loving arms.

The family traveled to Washington, where John Frémont was again hailed as a hero. When Jessie and John finished the report, he became known as "The Pathfinder," and her defiance of the government paid off. The grit of an 18-year-old girl and the bravery of her husband opened the West to immigration.

1 **A Man Unafraid**, by Herbert Bashford and Harr Wagner

John's third expedition was to survey Oregon and to secure California for the United States. Jessie helped with the preparations, but she also had absorbing work of her own. She was translating confidential literature for Secretary of State James Buchanan. Because he couldn't speak Spanish, he trusted Jessie to handle all his Mexican correspondence with the Southwest. Through the correspondence and from the newspapers, Jessie learned of her husband's involvement in the Bear Flag revolt.

When Frémont left on the expedition in 1844, he was the man in charge. While in California in 1846 the Mexicans ordered Frémont to withdraw. Instead he raised the flag! Two months later, when the United States and Mexico declared war, Frémont and a rag-tag band of settlers attacked a Mexican fort at Sonoma. They took the fort and then unfurled a homemade flag bearing a single star, a grizzly bear, and the words "California Republic." Although Frémont thought he had the authority to take such action, he was told he had disobeyed orders. Because of this, he was placed under arrest by General Stephen Watts Kearny and returned to Washington to face a court-martial. While the government condemned Frémont, the newspapers declared that the raising of the Bear Flag showed great courage — he temporarily became a hero in the eyes of the people.

Jessie was horrified by the events. She knew John had experienced a sensitive, insecure childhood which left him vulnerable when he received what he perceived to be a slight, and he would respond by fighting back. Her only thought was to go to him. She hired a boat and went up the Missouri River alone to a small place called Kansas City, where she stayed in a log cabin awaiting her husband's return. When Frémont arrived he was under arrest and had been forced to march behind Kearny's troops. Humiliated and wearing a Mexican sombrero with a scarlet sash, Frémont came haggard and defeated to his Jessie. His beard and hair were sprinkled with gray. The couple returned to Washington together, with Jessie close by Frémont's side.

In Washington, the explosive Senator Benton took over his son-in-law's defense. Although it was a dark time in the Frémonts' life, Jessie, at the age of 23, refused to wear black. She had just found out she was pregnant, and she would not bow to defeat. Jessie went to the courtroom wearing a red dress and sat in the audience with her head held high.

It was a sensational trial. Frémont's friend, Kit Carson, stood with him throughout the court-martial. Despite Benton's fight, Frémont was found guilty of disobedience and innocent of mutiny. He was released from arrest to report for duty. Jessie was stunned — Frémont was enraged! He wanted justice, not a slap; so John Frémont resigned his commission. It is interesting to note that when the Mexicans surrendered, they did so to Frémont, who had prepared a carefully drawn treaty ensuring the Native Californians their rights. The treaty was never implemented.

Frémont's next expedition to the Pacific was promoted by private funds raised by Senator Benton. Months earlier John had secured a 40,000-acre land grant in the Sierra Nevada Mountains southeast of San Francisco. It was called "Las Mariposas," which means "the butterflies." Following the expedition, Frémont planned to settle with his family and become a rancher on his land in California. It meant Jessie would not be left behind; she could go with her husband, but only after the baby was born.

The birth of her second child, however, affected Jessie's health. She had endured so much during the court-martial that her body had become weak, and her lungs were infected. When their son was born, he lived only a short while.

Distraught over the loss of her baby, and alarmed by the perils that lay ahead, Jessie nevertheless continued with her plans. Her love for John was stronger than her fear of leaving behind all she treasured. She had never been on her own. Everything would be new and strange. Tales of gold nuggets were filtering in from California where, it was said, a man could become rich in a week. Masses of fortune-seekers were scrambling to get to the "Golden State." This would make her trip even harder, as almost everyone had gold fever.

Senator Benton said his farewell to Jessie and Lily in New York. Since it would be unheard of for them to travel alone across the isthmus of Panama, he arranged for her older sister's husband, Richard Jacob, to accompany them. The senator also engaged a middle-age woman as a servant. It was a mistake, however, for she turned out to be a thief. Jacob later became ill and had to return home.

The journey was fraught with danger, and Jessie and Lily became thin and wan. Panama was filled with disease, extreme jungle heat, and the smell of rotting food. It was certainly not a place for a lone woman and her child. They were carried aboard a small steamer at Changres, transferred to a dugout canoe, then placed on the backs of mules for a 21-mile ride over the isthmus. Everyone begged Jessie to turn back, but she chose to go on.

The trip became a nightmare. When Jessie reached Panama City, she found the ship "California" had been abandoned in San Francisco. The crew had gone to find gold! Newspapers carried stories of Frémont's expedition, claiming he had been killed crossing the Rockies. Jessie clung to her faith and remained in Panama City. She was invited to stay with the aunt of the minister from Granada while awaiting the ship. Then the rains came, and water flowed down the inner walls of the house. Jessie became extremely ill. Her lung problem returned. She was delirious and hemorrhaging from her lungs. However, by the time the California finally arrived she had almost recovered. When the ship docked in San Francisco, John was not there, so Jessie and Lily were taken to a hotel. Ten days later, a frantic John Frémont arrived.

At that time, San Francisco was the main source of goods for the mines and the city was in chaos. Houses were at a premium in 1849, so Frémont took his family to Monterey, where they set up housekeeping in the wing of the big adobe occupied by the governor. It was comfortable, with thick walls and rose-bordered gardens. Jessie began to mend. Despite the lack of convenience, the family enjoyed being together and their future looked promising. Jessie learned to cook and clean and found no need for servants. She was no longer a pampered young wife afraid to go out on her own. With this new freedom it would be difficult to return to the narrow-minded life she left behind.

Fremont was becoming one of the most popular men in California: he was gaining wealth; his land continued to yield a rich supply of gold; and, he was married to Senator Benton's daughter.

At the same time, California was in turmoil and needed a leader. Because John spent a great deal of time supervising his mines in Las Mariposas, Jessie was surprised when he appeared at her bedside late one night. He had ridden 70 miles to tell her he had been elected senator of California, and they had to leave immediately for Washington.

The journey over the isthmus was another long ordeal, and at one time Jessie had to be strapped to a sofa and carried for her own safety. It was said by all laws of nature she should have died . Once back in Washington, Jessie looked at her thin figure and shabby clothing and decided a shopping trip was in order. But even fancy new clothes could not hide her pale face and the circles beneath her eyes.

The big issue for California in 1849 was slavery. John, Jessie, and Senator Benton were against it. Many politicians wanted to split the state, with the North free and the South having slaves. Frémont would not hear of it. He wanted even more than emancipation — he wanted justice and equal rights. The people in favor of slavery argued that the Frémonts would be the richest people in California if they let slaves run their mines. But the Frémonts' decision was on the side of paid labor. Jessie wanted to free all slaves. Because she had learned to do her own housework, she knew that society women did not need slaves. Jessie found herself speaking to congressmen and newspaper reporters, something she would never have considered doing before. She told them her father had refused two large inheritances because he would have had to take the slaves with the land. Her fiery speeches were like her father's, explosive at times but always controlled.

When they returned to California, Jessie was four months pregnant. Since her husband had drawn the short Senate term, it had expired. While he supervised Las Mariposas and became involved in more ways to make money, Jessie was busy being a mother. Her third child, John Charles, was a healthy, lovable baby. The family took a trip to Paris to celebrate his birth, and once again Jessie found she was expecting. The fourth child, Anne, died shortly after birth. John took the loss of this daughter with more emotion than his wife, and they left Paris to return to Washington.

In 1853, when Jessie was 29, Frémont went on another expedition and Jessie had her last child, Frank Preston. She realized Mr. Frémont would always need a new challenge or mountain to climb and she would always remain in the background, keeping their family together.

Her mother, Elizabeth, died soon after Frémont's departure, leaving Senator Benton grief-stricken. Jessie had her hands full as she cared for her children and consoled her father. Once again Benton and his daughter drew close in their sorrow. They didn't know it then, but it would be their last moments of companionship, for a few months later there would be a rift that would separate them for life.

Upon Frémont's return, he found that the people wanted him to become involved in politics. He was asked to accept the nomination for the candidacy as the president of the first "free soil, free speech, free press" Republican Party. After careful consideration the Frémonts accepted the opportunity. Senator Benton, however, refused to go along with their plans. He opposed the new Republican Party and Frémont's role in it. Jessie believed that her husband should run, and she defied her father to stand beside Frémont. She was an aspiring woman, and with her background Jessie thought she could help John win the presidency.

During the campaign Jessie Benton Frémont became the first woman to be involved in a presidential election. They were to run on an anti-slavery platform; and although John Frémont was the candidate, the people loved his wife. At rallies they carried signs that read "Frémont and Jessie," not "Frémont and Dayton," his running mate. Jessie came as close as any woman of that era would to the center of power. The words "Our Jessie" were frequently used along with John Frémont's name. When he received the candidacy, cheering crowds would not leave the front of their hotel until Jessie appeared on the balcony. Songs were written about her; women wore violet, her favorite color; and baby girls were named Jessie Ann.

Jessie took care of all of her husband's correspondence and constantly entertained important people. She always protected John from any unfavorable news or reports. She was still watching over her insecure husband while attempting to remain in the background for the sake of appearances.

Eventually Frémont's birth became an issue during the campaign, and lies were spread about his wife. Senator Benton blasted his own son-in-law, breaking Jessie's heart. Being caught between two men she dearly loved was difficult. When she chose her husband over her father, she added fuel to Benton's speeches. Had Benton stood behind Frémont, he might have won the election; but the senator turned his back, hurting the one person he loved, his daughter. When James Buchanan won the presidential election, it was Jessie who suffered the most.

Following the unsuccessful election, the Frémonts returned to California and Las Mariposas. It was time to leave politics behind. They moved into a little adobe house in Bear Valley. It was surrounded by geraniums, and Jessie added several log buildings to increased its size to accommodate her family. They painted the house white and called it the "White House." For the first time John settled down and became the head of his family. He even took an interest in his children, something he had never done before. Horace Greeley visited once, reminding them of his words, "Go West, young man," and tried to talk Frémont into re-entering politics. But John declined; he was happy. He loved the sunrises and would take a daily horseback ride, returning home to eat a hearty breakfast. In the summer they camped at Yosemite in a huge tent that opened on three sides, enjoying the grandeur of the mountains. Jessie said in her memoirs the two years spent at Bear Valley were the Frémonts' happiest. It ended, however, when there was a dispute over property rights, and mismanagement was draining the Frémonts' money.

In 1860 they moved to Black Point, on the cliffs overlooking San Francisco Bay, and John commuted to Las Mariposas. In 1861 Frémont accepted a commission as a Major General, commanding the Department of the West, and the family left for St. Louis. During his brief stay there, Frémont again met with opposition from the government when he issued a limited emancipation proclamation freeing the slaves of Missouri citizens fighting on the side of the Confederacy. He was also accused of incompetence in the manage-

ment of his troops. Although Frémont was called the great eman-
cipator, President Lincoln canceled his commission. John asked his
wife to visit the President on his behalf; but when she went to
Washington, Jessie was met with hostility. She returned defeated.
It was said the real reason John Frémont lost his commission was
that he represented a threat to President Lincoln.

The family then settled briefly in New York, but Frémont was
moody and withdrawn. Jessie decided to speak out on behalf of her
husband, and she wrote *The Story of the Guard* but didn't publish
it for fear of hurting John's chance for another command.

In 1864 Frémont relinquished control of Las Mariposas to a
company that left him with less money than he anticipated. In 1866
he became a partner in a railroad that had yet to be financed, but that
too fell apart. By 1867 the Frémonts were almost penniless, and
Jessie began writing for the *New York Ledger*, receiving $100 per
column. To spare her husband's feelings and minimize the fact they
needed money, she called her writing a "pastime." Frémont became
more depressed when he found out they did not have the money to
pay their taxes and everything of value had to be sold. They rented
a small house, and Jessie supported the family. She never condemned
her husband for his mistakes. She was writing for *Harper's
Magazine* and sold a book but still could not earn enough money.

In 1878 Frémont was appointed territorial governor of Arizona,
and they enjoyed four years of security. They moved in 1887 to Los
Angeles, where they couple worked together to publish John C.
Frémont's *Memoirs of My Life.* In 1890 he was restored to his
former rank of Major General, but he died two months later. At that
time all the Frémont children gathered to help their mother in her
grief. Jessie was lost without John — he was her life.

Lily remained with her mother; she never married and was
completely devoted to Jessie. The women of Los Angeles built
them a cottage in 1892; and in 1900 Jessie suffered a fractured hip,
becoming a semi-invalid. She eventually began to write again and
produced several articles, books, and her memoirs. Both mother
and daughter lived a quiet life until Jessie's death in 1902. She was
78 years old.

Jessie was cremated, and her ashes were packed in violets for burial beside her beloved John at Rocklin Cemetery in Hudson, New York, overlooking the Hudson River.

Jessie Benton Frémont was a woman who left her mark in history. She lived a life of extremes and had it all — wealth and poverty, fame and obscurity — but most importantly, she shared a rare love that lasted almost a century.

For a detailed account of Jessie Benton Frémont's life, the author highly recommends the book "Jessie Benton Frémont" *by Pamela Herr.*

PETTED BY OLD HICKORY

One of her first political friends was President Jackson, and one of her earliest recollections was being taken to the White House by her father and remaining with him and the President while they had their talks. It pleased Jackson to have her near him, where he could put his hand on her head, and sometimes, in the interest of discussion, he would forget what he was doing and take an unconscious grip on the pretty curls, but the little lady never winced. To have shown pain or displeasure would have displeased her father, who always praised her afterward when she was brave, and managed to have her rewarded at the time by a play in the nursery with the children of the President's niece, who lived with him.

Mrs. Fremont made her social debut at the White House at the age of 13, when President Van Buren gave a dinner for his son, and at 14 she attended a great state dinner given by the President in honor of the Russian Minister, Bodisco, the Splendid, and his 16-year-old bride. This remarkable marriage of May and December (the bridegroom was 65) was the most gorgeous ceremony Washington had ever seen. The bridal party was composed of the most beautiful of youthful girl friends of the bride and men of about the age of the groom. Jessie Benton, then 14, was one of the bridesmaids, with Mr. Buchanan, afterward President, as her grooms-man. The other groomsmen were distinguished men in official life, and the bride was given away by Henry Clay.

In this way began a brilliant social career which brought her in contact with such women of the past as Mrs. Alexander Hamilton and Mrs. Dolly Madison and all the prominent people of her father's day and generation.

Excerpted from Jessie Benton Frémont's obituary in the San Francisco Chronicle, December 28, 1902, courtesy of the Mariposa Historical Society.

General John C. Frémont

Jessie Benton Frémont, the wife of John C. Frémont

*The Frémonts' home in Bear Valley which was a part
of the Las Mariposas land grant*

Jessie Benton Frémont was a woman who bore her triumps without arrogance and her defeats without bitterness.

Abigail Scott Duniway

Chapter 2

ABIGAIL SCOTT DUNIWAY
✦ ✦
"The Grand Old Lady of Oregon"

W ith less than a sixth-grade education, Abigail Duniway became a noted journalist and prominent suffragist who gained recognition as a dedicated leader for women's rights. She endured hardship, deprivation, ridicule, and sneers as she fought a 42-year battle to achieve her goal, becoming the first woman in Oregon to register to vote in a national election. Because of her tireless efforts, Oregon became the seventh state to allow women the right to vote, eight years before the passing of the 19th Amendment.

On October 22, 1834, the day that Abigail Jane Scott entered this world, her mother wept and her father was angry, for another daughter *"was almost too grievous to be borne."*[1] She was the second daughter and third child of Ann and John Tucker Scott. Their first child, a boy, had died in infancy, and Abigail started her life as a burden before she drew her first breath in the little log cabin in Tazewell County, Illinois.

During the early years of Abigail's life, Illinois suffered severe flooding followed by a drought. The farming families endured disease, short crops, and an overabundance of insects. The wives were so busy scratching a living from the unyielding land that there was barely time to care for a baby. Abigail's earliest recollections were of sitting on the cluttered floor, surrounded by flies, sucking on a piece of bacon attached by a string to the bed post.

As Abigail grew into a frail, skinny little girl, she learned the true meaning of the word "work." It didn't matter how hard the task or how small the child, everyone had to contribute to the family's never-ending chores. In her diary, Abigail wrote that although adults believed no child was in danger from overwork, she thought

1 **Rebel for Rights,** by Ruth Barnes Moynihan

it was a fatal misconception. It was in her case, as through all her life, Abigail was to suffer from illness and a chronic weakness of the spine. In later years she developed painful rheumatoid arthritis, eventually becoming a cripple.

Abigail watched her overworked, sickly mother bear nine more children over the years. The six girls and three boys seemed to arrive about every 18 months, and each one meant more food to raise and extra work for everyone. Her childhood memories included standing on a chair washing dishes, paring huge piles of apples, and spending tedious hours going over wool fleece. She hated every minute of it and was filled with resentment. Abigail soon became known as the rebel daughter. She had a fast temper and lived in a dream world, hating domesticity, yet fearing the wrath of Hell's fire and brimstone that was preached from the pulpit every Sunday.

The child dearly loved her family, especially her strong, intelligent father. Although he demanded respect and ruled the family, John Tucker was a fair man who constantly encouraged Abigail to study and write in her spare time. Next to her father, she adored her younger brother Harvey, who was Abigail's responsibility. They played together, and later in life both became editors and writers. Harvey, however, was never to support Abigail's suffragist beliefs. His opposition to her cause often hindered his sister's success, and through the years their sibling rivalry grew into many verbal battles. Toward her mother, Abigail felt pity and looked upon her as an overworked invalid, someone she had no desire to imitate.

Abigail's first academic lessons were at home with her grandmother, where they spent what few spare hours they shared studying Webster's Spelling book. The young girl was a fast learner and soon began to spell, read, and recite poetry. Words became Abigail's life. She read every newspaper and magazine she could find, and became so proficient at writing that many of her early verses were published in the county newspaper.

At the age of 8, Abigail attended the local school for a few months, but her frail health prevented a full semester. Later in 1850 when she was 16, her father sent her to a small academy for a year, until again ill health forced Abigail to leave. While at the academy she heard the first whispers about women's rights and learned of suffragist Elizabeth Cady Stanton. She also read about Horace Greeley and agreed with him that slavery should not be allowed. Both Stanton and Greeley became role models who helped to form Abigail's future.

The Scott family was a large clan almost 100 strong. There were cousins, aunts, and uncles all over Tazewell County. They were deep-thinking, strong-willed people with a tendency to be work-oriented. Although Abigail did not respect authority and hated discipline, she fulfilled her tasks and easily made friends among the children. Abigail was considered the intellectual in the family; and as she entered womanhood, she became an outspoken individual who was known for her beautiful poetry and sharp wit.

By 1845 the rough highway in front of the Scotts' farm had become the main emigrant route. Year after year the family watched the parade of covered wagons heading West. Tucker Scott would go out to meet the travelers, learning everything he could about Oregon. They told of the freedom, space, fertile soil, and beauty of the country. Over the years John Tucker collected every bit of written information he could find. In 1850, when the Oregon Donation Land Act entitled every man 320 acres of land and another 320 if he had a wife, Abigail's father decided to move his family West. There were nine living children in the Scott family, and their mother had become a semi-invalid from years of childbearing and overwork. Tucker believed she would regain her health in the Oregon climate, and since no one dared to refuse him, the family started planning for the long trip. His timid wife cried and begged Tucker not to go, but he declared she was being a foolish woman.

During the winter of 1851, everyone pitched in to prepare for the long journey. The women and girls made extra blankets, bedding, clothing, and a large feather bed for Tucker and his wife Ann to sleep upon. Every unnecessary item was sold or auctioned off, including Abigail's precious books. The only two things she managed to keep were a small spelling book, which she hid in the bottom of her sewing basket, and six Dutch plates that her mother prized. The plates were carefully stored in the feather mattress.

On April 2, 1852, the family took its place among the long line of covered wagons. As they headed out, almost everyone except Tucker was crying. He had planned the trip carefully, with $2,000 hidden away and five new wagons pulled by sturdy oxen and horses. His spirits were high, and so were Abigail's. She was very excited and looked upon the trip as a great adventure, allowing her freedom from the drudgery of the farm. The Scotts didn't know at that time they were part of the largest migration in history, and they had no idea of the tragedies, shortages, and illness that lay ahead.

The party was filled with optimism and cheer as it left Illinois. The Scotts were soon joined by other families and their wagons on their way to Oregon, which was called the "Eden of the West." The last thing Abigail saw as they turned the corner was her grandfather's tears as he leaned against the fence, waving farewell with an old red handkerchief. There was no turning back for the party of 11 Scotts, 16 members of their immediate family, and the few young men accompanying them as drivers. Abigail had been selected by her father to keep the daily journal, an honor that made her feel quite important.

The first part of the trip went smoothly. Space was limited as the wagons were filled with necessities for the journey. The younger children rode with their mothers who sat on small chairs in cramped quarters. Abigail and her sisters walked most of the way, occasionally hitching a ride on one of the horses as the wagons rolled along to the West. They first saw slaves in Missouri, which upset the family and filled Abigail with fury. Her free soul shook with anger at the thought of one person being owned by another. She vowed to work toward their freedom, calling slavery a blight upon the nation.

Several weeks into the journey things began to get serious. They encountered hailstorms and dust storms, quicksand, and overflowing rivers where a young driver was drowned. Later, disease became rampant and many suffered from colds and constant diarrhea. All feared cholera, which had reached epidemic proportions. On June 20, Abigail's mother fell ill with the dreaded disease, and in her frail condition she soon bid her family farewell. They sadly buried her beside the trail in a small grave that had to be covered with rocks to keep the wild animals away. Her daughters surrounded the site with wildflowers, and the party moved on toward the West.

In August, death again visited the Scotts when 3-1/2-year-old Willie Scott also died of cholera, and another small grave was left by the side of the Oregon Trail. Soon after, most of their wagons had to be discarded, and Tucker's $2,000 had long been spent. The girls were all barefoot, their feet sore and swollen from sharp rocks and briars along the trail. With the older ones carrying the smaller children, Tucker Scott finally led what was left of his family to the "promised land." They were ragged, weary and poor, having been on the trail for six months. Abigail would always remember the two small graves they left behind and how a man could impose his will on an unwilling wife.

Following their arrival in Oregon, the Scotts were assisted by relatives who had successfully made the journey. They spent the first few months in a rented building which Tucker Scott turned into a hotel called The Oregon Temperance House. The "hired" help consisted of his daughters with the exception of Abigail, who had no desire to resume a life of drudgery. She became a teacher in a tiny log cabin school in the small community of Eola. Abigail had grown into an attractive young woman who frequently spent her nights studying to keep ahead of her students. Her father married a healthy 25-year-old widow with two children. It had barely been eight months since he buried his first wife Ann, and his children were shocked.

The Donation Land Act had become an important issue in Oregon. Desperate bachelors frantically combed the countryside looking for wives so they could acquire the 320 acres for themselves and an extra 320 acres for being married. The law, however, did not say that the wife would ever own the land; it merely stated that married men would receive 640 acres free of charge. Since there were few single women in Oregon, every available female from the age of 14 to 80 was courted. This made Abigail one of the most eligible young women in the area. She was a sparkling 18-year-old who overnight had more suitors than she could handle.

Abigail had sought to be independent all of her young life, and the mate she would choose could not be a domineering, insensitive man. After several proposals, she finally selected Benjamin C. Duniway, a gentle, warmhearted man who was respected by the community. It was a whirlwind courtship, followed by a simple ceremony in which Abigail omitted the word "obey" and declined the 320 acres of land, declaring she was Ben's choice because he loved her, not the land. Ben agreed to whatever Abigail desired.

Following the wedding Abigail and Ben claimed his 320 acres of land on the timbered banks of a creek in the loneliness of Clackamas County, Oregon. It was an untamed wilderness that was excellent for hunting but difficult to farm. Abigail immediately became pregnant, and on this sparse piece of land she again became a slave to men. Without planning to do so, Abigail found herself walking the same footsteps as her mother, as much a captive as Ann Scott had been. There were always hired hands to feed, and Ben's many bachelor friends constantly dropped by for Abigail's tasty home-cooked meals. Her work was endless: cooking, washing, weaving, and child-rearing when her daughter Clara was born. Abigail helped Ben clear the land, and in her spare time raised chickens for eggs and churned butter to take to the market for spending money. However, she never saw one penny from the eggs and butter; Ben kept it all in his pocket. In her discontent, Abigail began calling their homestead "Hardscrabble."

Abigail's second child Willis was born less than two years after Clara. It was a long, hard delivery with only neighbors and a midwife assisting. Following Willis' birth, Abigail remained a semi-invalid for several months. To occupy her active mind, she started writing poetry; she wrote with one foot upon the cradle-rocker, and her sisters came to help with the endless chores. With Ben's encouragement, she sent her poetry to the *Oregon Argus*, and to Abigail's delight, it was accepted. At the age of 22 she became a regular contributor to the paper, writing under the name of "Jenny Glen."

While Abigail was struggling for survival at Hardscrabble, her brother Harvey was attending college. He went on to become a librarian in the Portland, Oregon, Library and furthered his education at Pacific University. Both brother and sister were highly intelligent, but Abigail was still the little girl whose birth was a grievance to her parents. Girls were not expected to become scholars, and the majority never did.

In 1855 Abigail and Ben left their homestead and moved to Yamhill County, where Ben hoped to become a successful farmer. There, Abigail was considered an intellectual and enjoyed the society of other enterprising women. Life was considerably kinder to her. The bachelors no longer visited at mealtime, so she had only her family and hired hands to care for. Although the constant chores of being a farmer's wife were still a burden, Abigail found time to expand her writing talents and began a novel based on her Oregon journal. She also gave birth to her third child, Hubert. The Duniway family was happy, and Abigail called their new home "Sunny Hillside."

Her novel, *Captain Gray's Company, or Crossing the Plains and Living in Oregon,* was published In 1859 when Abigail was 25. It was the first commercially printed novel in Oregon. Unfortunately the book was a failure. It received unfavorable reviews, and Abigail was criticized for the use of bad grammar, poor dialogue, and too many characters depicted as abused, overworked women. Abigail was devastated and spent the rest of her life apologizing for the book. However, she was not one to give up easily and began writing *The Farmer's Wife,* a column for the *New Oregon Farmer.* It was a controversial piece which exposed the drudgery and problems of the farmers' wives and elicited a considerable amount of agitation among the male population. Abigail, who was no longer easily crushed, fought back, becoming more interested in women's issues and politics.

During this period, Oregon entered a depression, and Abigail gave birth to her fourth child, Wilkie. She helped Ben supplement their income with her writing and again began selling eggs and butter. It was a hard period in the family's life, which became worse when a friend of Ben's could not repay notes for which Ben had co-signed. Abigail had begged her husband to not sign the notes, but as a woman she did not have the right to make a decision. Ben had soothed her with the promise that he would always protect and provide for their family. In desperation he was forced to find work in the Oregon mines, leaving Abigail and the children behind.

While he was gone, the sheriff served the summons for the notes to Abigail who was furious because she became responsible for the amount due. When Ben returned, there was no way they could keep their land, so they lost Sunny Hillside.

In 1863, when Abigail was 28, the Duniways moved into the only property they still owned, a small house in Lafayette. Abigail soon turned it into a school, something she had always wanted to do. She was free of the drudgery of the farm and became part of the intellectual world she admired. To increase their income, Abigail made the attic into a dormitory for boarding students. It was a tireless task. Abigail had to rise at 3 a.m. to do the household chores and cooking, then taught school all day; but she was content.

For the first time in his life Ben was forced to look for work, and after a fruitless search started his own hauling business. That, too, was a failure. He was injured when his team bolted, throwing him under the wheels. Ben was to remain a semi-invalid the rest of his life. This added more to Abigail's already full schedule, but the family pulled together and survived. Ben was able to care for their children and help with the housework, and in 1865 Abigail sold the school for a profit. She opened a new one in Albany, Oregon, and Ben was able to resume his business part-time.

The next year Abigail found she was again expecting and, because teaching was too hard, she established a small millinery shop. With only $30 in her purse, the intrepid Mrs. Duniway took the steamboat to Portland. She hoped to buy her stock with a minimal down payment, putting the rest on credit. The wholesaler, however, was so impressed with her ambition that he insisted on selling Abigail $1,200 worth of goods, which she repaid within three weeks. The millinery shop was a financial success, and the Duniways were no longer poor.

Although the business was going well, Abigail still wanted to be a writer. She was envious of her brother Harvey, who was now the editor of the *Portland Oregonian*, a very influential newspaper. Abigail knew that she too could have been an editor if she had the chance. In her millinery shop — surrounded by ribbons, lace, ruffles, and fancy little bonnets — Abigail began to learn of the plight of other women. She was soon writing about them. The sufferings of these women was pitiful. One mother had been deserted by her husband who sold all their household items and left town. She needed to borrow money to rent a house and buy furniture so she could support herself and children by taking in boarders. Abigail told a friend, and he loaned the woman the money with the furniture as chattel. The woman established herself and was doing well until her husband returned, rejected the loan, and sold the furniture — all of which was legal because women did not have rights.

Another sickly wife of a wealthy farmer begged for a sewing job to buy her daughters' waterproof coats. She had diligently saved the butter money which was taken from her by her husband to purchase a race horse. Abigail could not hire the woman but offered to make the coats on credit, which the wife was afraid to accept. The next summer when the wife died during childbirth, the pious clergymen offered condolences to the bereaved husband; and again Abigail wondered at the injustices dealt to women.

The stories were always the same — abuse, overwork, and deprivation. Mrs. Duniway's heart went out to these unfortunate human beings, and her crusading spirit began to stir. She helped all she could and let her pen tell their stories, one of which she submitted to her brother Harvey, who refused to print it.

Abigail had two more children during these years. The last delivery was so difficult that she was told not to have any more children and was forced to occasionally wear "artificial aids." Abigail's health was in danger. She was in almost constant pain, yet her spirit was never stronger. Ben accepted the doctor's orders as he was an understanding man, and Abigail remained a dutiful wife in all ways except one. She continued with her writing and the millinery shop.

One day Abigail was asked to accompany a friend to the courthouse. The woman's husband had died without a will and she could not get enough of his estate on which to live. On their way to the courthouse, which was an all-male establishment, the woman told Abigail that she and her girls had sold butter, eggs, cord-wood, vegetables, and grain. They had also worked the farm to meet the never-ending bills. The court, however, would not let her have enough of the estate to buy a pair of shoestrings. If the woman had died before her spouse, all the money they had earned in 20 years would have gone to her husband to spend as he saw fit. Abigail was so outraged that she went home to Ben and told him the story, saying, *"One half of the women are dolls, the rest of them drudges, and we're all fools."*

Ben placed his hand on her head and told her that women would never be better off until they had the right to vote. When Abigail asked what good that would do, Ben told her that women do half the work of the world and if women were voters, there would soon be lawmakers among them. Then Abigail realized what had to be done, and she found her mission in life. Filled with burning ambition, the mother of six became an ambitious suffragist who would spend the rest of her life building a better world for women.

Abigail had never been a journalist, but she resolved to publish a weekly newspaper for women. The Duniways moved to Portland, where Mrs. Duniway rented the upper floor of a two-story house to be used as a print shop. She hired a man who would produce the paper, and she planned to teach her sons to run the business. In 1871 *The New Northwest* was born. Under the masthead it carried the motto "Free Speech, Free Press, Free People." Abigail wrote the editorial copy, and her newspaper had something for everyone. She dispensed sympathy and advice in her correspondence column, where her writing was lively and to the point. To one nervous sufferer she recommended rest, and to another she suggested he stop blubbering. She developed schemes for fallen women and pressed for reform. Abigail was formidable and always alert for the feminist angle.

When suffragists Susan B. Anthony and Elizabeth Cady Stanton were lecturing in the West, Abigail invited them to Portland to do a series of lectures. Miss Anthony accepted; and although Mrs. Duniway had been fearful of the outspoken woman, she found her to be soft-spoken and friendly. However, it was difficult to find a place to hold the lectures as even the churches refused them entrance. Finally Abigail rented a hall, where Ben collected tickets and their daughter Clara provided the music.

Abigail introduced the noted Miss Anthony in such a warm,

gracious manner that she received more invitations to speak than she could accept, and soon Abigail was speaking out for women's rights. During one of her lectures an amusing incident occurred when a man refuted her argument for suffrage by saying, *"I have often known a hen to try to crow, but I've never seen one yet."* The sharp-tongued Abigail replied, *"In the poultry yard of my friend in Albany, I once saw a rooster try to set, and he made a failure too."[1]* It was said the man never again attended one of Mrs. Duniway's lectures.

Following the Portland meetings, Miss Anthony and Mrs. Duniway visited the Oregon back-country by stage, wagon, or horseback. They continued on to Washington, speaking in dirty halls, the back rooms of saloons, and an occasional church. Wherever they appeared they spoke of injustices, claiming that most wives were more or less slaves. Anthony and Duniway were accused of being alcoholics and of being immoral, and were often pelted with rotten eggs, but they went on crusading. When Abigail returned to Portland, she was a seasoned campaigner eager to continue her cause in the state of Oregon. She had lectured her way across the country many times and faithfully sent columns to *The New Northwest*, which carried accounts of her travels. Ben and Clara took care of the children while Abigail was gone.

With a successful tour behind her, Abigail started lobbying on behalf of women's rights. As A. J. Duniway, she was well-known through her newspaper and found rapport with the lawmakers. In 1872 she was allowed to introduce a suffrage bill before the Washington Legislature. Although the bill did not pass, she did gain approval for the "Sole Trader Bill," which enabled a woman engaged in business to register the fact with the county clerk, thereby protecting her tools, furniture, and stock from seizure by her husband's creditors. The legislation also added that in the event a husband abandoned his wife, she could obtain the court's permission to sell or lease property, make contracts, and collect money due him.

When the temperance movement became an issue in Oregon, Abigail immediately became affiliated with the society. She thought it would provide an opportunity for her to reach more people

---

1 Excerpts from **Elizah Lafayette Bristow's** letter, Oregon Historical Society

through the churches as they preached the evils of alcohol. Sunday after Sunday she attended services, but the pastor repeatedly stopped her from speaking. The outspoken A. J. Duniway, however, got her chance one Sunday when she sat in the front pew waiting for a lull in the service. When it finally arrived Abigail, with her customary revolutionary zeal, sprang to her feet and shouted, "Let us pray," then successfully delivered a 20-minute speech while the irritated pastor stood by silently, knowing he could not interrupt a prayer.

Later Abigail realized the temperance movement would not benefit suffrage. She knew most men would never support Prohibition which would take away their freedom. Since men made the laws, they would not help to achieve women's rights if they had to give up one of their own. She declared she was opposed to the prohibition party and started writing editorials, claiming that alcoholism was a physical problem, not a moral evil.

Meanwhile the suffrage movement was growing in the Washington Territory. Abigail was allowed to address the Legislature there, and again her eloquence and dramatic appeal were successful. In 1883 the suffrage bill was passed in Washington. She hurried home, certain that during the next year the suffrage amendment would pass in Oregon. A. J. Duniway and her followers conducted a full-scale campaign. They spoke at conventions and held a rally in Salem, where Abigail told the women they were classed below lunatics, idiots, and criminals because even the lowest bum could vote and the women could not. In the end it was all in vain; her amendment lost in 1884. She not only lost the amendment that year; she lost her daughter Clara, who died at the age of 31. The following year Ben became very ill and Abigail sold her beloved newspaper, *The New Northwest*, claiming she had lost another child.

The Duniways bought a large ranch in Idaho, hoping that Ben would regain his health in the pure, clean air. Once she had established the family, Abigail found the Idaho women desperately struggling to pass suffrage. She picked up her banner and moved in to help, often returning to the home in Portland where she wrote to supplement the family's income. In 1896 Idaho followed the lead of Wyoming and Colorado, granting women the right to vote. Later that year Ben Duniway quietly passed away. In one of her columns, his wife fondly remembered his loyalty to her and reminded the women of Oregon how much he had given to their cause.

After Ben's death, A. J. Duniway threw herself into politics. She fought her brother Harvey and his anti-suffrage newspaper, both vocally and in writing. Abigail founded women's clubs, led parades, and held rallies; and in 1906 the amendment was again placed on the Oregon ballot. It lost by a small margin. In 1908 she borrowed money and tried again. Each time her support grew stronger, and A. J. Duniway grew more determined. When she lost the 1910 battle, everyone said Abigail was finished. At the age of 76 she spent most of her time in a wheelchair, and her treasury was empty; but Abigail's spirit was as strong as ever.

The undaunted woman had spent almost her entire life working to achieve the women's right to vote — she wasn't going to give up now! By 1911 she had outlived her brother Harvey and gained the support of his newspaper, *The Oregonian*. A. J. Duniway worked from her home, using other people's legs to carry the campaign forward. During her last speeches, Abigail claimed that when she went to heaven, she wanted to go as a free woman, and she did. "The Grand Old Lady of Oregon" won her battle for the vote in 1912, a few days after her 78th birthday. When interviewed, Abigail claimed she was content. Governor Oswald West personally invited Abigail Scott Duniway to inscribe the official proclamation of the constitutional amendment. When she proudly appeared at the polls as the first woman in Oregon to cast a vote, A. J. Duniway arrived appropriately dressed in lavender and lace.

Following her victory, Abigail continued to write and work for worthy causes. In 1915, just before her 81st birthday, this high-spirited woman passed away. She will always be respected and admired as a notable Western lady who spent 42 years working to gain the right for every woman to vote. One of her favorite pieces of advice was "Do not yield to difficulties, but rise above discouragements."

*Abigail Scott Duniway holding a copy of her
newspaper **The New Northwest***

◆————————————————————————————◆—·

Abigail Scott Duniway registering to vote

She was the first woman registered to vote
in the Oregon election of 1912.

Princess Sarah Winnemucca

Chapter 3

SARAH WINNEMUCCA

The Sagebrush Princess

S arah Winnemucca will always be remembered as a dedicated Native American woman who belonged to two cultures. With one foot in the Indian Nation and the other in the white man's world, she sped across the plains like a blazing arrow, only to fall short of her target. Although the Princess was recognized throughout the land as the passionate voice of the Paiute Indians, she was treated with indifference by the United States government. Disillusioned and betrayed, Sarah died before she completed her mission, believing herself to be a failure.

Before the appearance of the white man, the Northern Paiute Indians freely roamed the high deserts of northwestern Nevada, northeastern California and southeastern Oregon. It was a large peaceful tribe, divided into bands, each with its own leader or chief. The Paiutes' lives were spent hunting and gathering throughout their territory, where they endured the fierce winter storms and swirling dust in a land where food was scarce. The Paiutes called themselves the numa, which meant "people," and they were happy — because they were free.

In 1844 Sarah Winnemucca was born into this tribe. Her parents named her Thocmentony, an Indian name for "shell-flower." She was the fourth child and second daughter of Chief Winnemucca. Her grandfather was the famous Chief Truckee, also known as Captain Truckee, a name bestowed upon him by General John C. Frémont for his help in the Bear War against Mexican control of California.

While Truckee was gone for months at a time working as a guide for the white emigrants, his son-in-law Winnemucca served as a sub-chief. They were good leaders, having no wish to raid or pillage, only desiring a peaceful co-existence with others. The various tribes would wander for weeks or months without seeing each other. When they came together it was a time for celebration, gossip, courtship, and a meeting of their leaders. During one of these celebrations Sarah's younger sister Elma was born.

When Captain Truckee returned from his trips he was always a welcome sight. The old chief would sit for hours entertaining the children with tales of his white brothers. He told of their fine homes, fancy clothes, and abundance of food. During these visits Truckee would proudly display his "rag-friend," a letter of commendation from General Frémont. Although the captain trusted the white men and called them his brothers, Winnemucca was of a different opinion. He had no faith in the word of the white men, and he attempted to remain as far as possible from them.

The little golden-skinned girl, who dearly loved her grandfather, would listen to the two chiefs discuss the issue of these strange men. At that time, she didn't realize the influence their conversations would have upon her future. Sarah adored her grandfather, and because of his admiration for the white men, she believed they couldn't be all bad.

In the spring of 1850, when Sarah was 6 years old, Captain Truckee returned to his people with plans to move the Paiutes to California so they could learn the ways of his white brothers. Winnemucca, along with the majority of the tribe, refused to accompany Truckee. The captain, however, was so enthusiastic that several families did agree to make the trip. At Truckee's insistence, his daughter and her children — including Sarah — were forced to go. Winnemucca remained behind to take care of the tribe when the small party left for California.

At first the sight of so many white faces, with their beards and light-colored eyes, frightened the child. However, her fear soon turned to amazement as her people passed through the larger cities and towns. Wherever Captain Truckee showed his rag-friend, everyone welcomed them. After several days of traveling, the small group eventually stopped at a large ranch near the San Joaquin River. The men were employed as ranch hands, and the women went to work in the big house. It was at this ranch that Sarah enjoyed the luxury of her first bed and tasted the white man's food. The little girl fell in love with the bright dishes in the kitchen, red-plush chairs, and fancy pictures on the walls. She also acquired the name of Sarah, because Thocmentony was too hard to pronounce.

Although the Paiutes appreciated their wages, which to them seemed a fortune, they did not like the way the white men treated them, especially the Indian wives and daughters. All was not as Truckee had promised. Most of the cowboys made rude remarks to the teen-age girls, and Sarah's older sister Mary suffered several unpleasant advances. They learned that it was not uncommon for the white men to force Indian women to become servants or to submit to their sexual desires. White women were scarce, and mixed marriages were illegal, so a few of the Indian women became common-law wives. They were never respected and were usually looked down upon.

Within a few months, Captain Truckee's little group had seen enough of the white man's ways. The Paiutes decided to return to their own territory and customs. While Sarah wanted to believe her beloved grandfather, she began to understand her father's distrust of the white men. As they left California, she carried many mixed emotions.

By 1851 the Northern Indians were in the way of progress. Hundreds of emigrants passed through the territory daily on their way to the rich gold fields in California. Many people remained to settle in Nevada, and small towns began to spring up in all directions. In order to find food, Truckee and Winnemucca were forced to take their people to the less populated high-country. During this period Sarah and her older brother Natchez became close friends. Natchez was a tall, handsome Paiute who believed in peaceful co-existence among people.

Truckee occasionally left the mountains to return to the world of his white brothers. He had a strong desire to see Sarah educated in their ways. The old man knew that one day these white men would rule the land, and for that reason, he wanted his favorite grandchild to live as they did.

On one of his frequent visits to the Mormon Station, later to be called Genoa, Captain Truckee arranged for Sarah and her younger sister Elma to work for a prominent citizen, Major Ormsby, and his wife. The Major owned a store and stage stop where the two girls could help with the customers and travelers. They would also perform household chores and serve as companions to the couple's 9-year-old daughter Lizzie.

In 1857 Sarah, at the age of 13, and her sister Elma became members of the Ormsby family. It was a valuable experience for the two girls who were used to running barefoot and wearing buckskins. The Ormsbys outfitted them from head to toe in colorful, long calico dresses with perky white collars and shoes with bright little buttons. They learned manners and the ways of the white settlers. By the time Sarah was 14, she could converse freely in English and Mexican, as well as three Indian dialects. She was considered an attractive Paiute girl and often attended square dances with the Ormsby family. Sarah was a sought-after partner who danced extremely well, although she always remained aloof and proud.

During their stay with the Ormsbys, the girls witnessed a very unpleasant event. Two Washoe Indians were accused of a crime they did not commit and were shot to death. Later it was discovered the crime had been perpetrated by two white men. This incident marked the beginning of many misunderstandings between the settlers and Indians, and again Sarah was reminded of her father's distrust of the white men.

Following the disturbance, Winnemucca sent Natchez to bring the two girls home. He was alarmed at the growing hostility, and the Indians lost what little faith they still had in the settlers. It was the worst winter the Paiutes could remember. Tension was high; many suffered from hunger and died. The white men did not respect the treaties and took control of tribal lands. The Paiutes were so distrustful they refused food sent by the settlers, fearing it was poisonous. When two Indian girls were reported missing, the problems became worse.

Members of the tribe were sent to look for the girls. When they found them in the basement at William's Station, the girls had been badly abused. A band of wandering Indians from another tribe avenged the girls' mistreatment by killing the two William brothers and burning their station. Soon other homes along the Carson River were attacked by the Indians, and a general uprising began. Winnemucca and his people did not take part in the violence; they attempted to negotiate a peaceful solution. When the warfare eventually ended, the settlers and Indians once more tried to live in harmony.

Shortly after the conflict, Captain Truckee became ill while gathering pine nuts with members of his tribe. He requested fire signals be built upon the mountain tops to summon the people, especially his precious granddaughter. Truckee knew the end was near. Because he had never lost his desire to see Sarah educated, he requested a white friend to take Sarah and Elma to the "sisters" at San Jose, California, so they could attend the convent school there. Then Truckee called his loved ones to his side for a last farewell and declared Winnemucca the official chief of the Paiutes. His last wish was to have his rag-friend placed upon his breast when they buried him. In Sarah's book, *Life Among the Paiutes,* written 28 years later, she wrote about her grandfather with genuine affection and told of his honesty and influence upon all those he met.

Following the burial rites, Truckee's friend kept his promise and arranged for Natchez to take the girls to San Jose. Sarah was 16 years old. As they rode through the camp she held her head high and hid the tears of sorrow for her grandfather that gathered in her eyes.

When the two girls arrived at the Convent of Notre Dame in San Jose, they created quite a furor, as they were the only Indians who had ever attempted to enroll in the school. The records at the convent do not show they were admitted, but it is believed that Sarah and Elma were there for several weeks. In her book, Sarah claims it was the happiest period in her life. She slept in a clean bed and learned fancy needlework along with the academics. Although the girls were fine students, they were not allowed to remain in the school due to white prejudice. The wealthy San Francisco matrons looked upon the Indians' presence as an offense to their own daughters. Natchez could not go to get them, so Sarah and Elma traveled home alone. This, however, did not end Sarah's education; she continued to learn on her own through persistence and determination.

Upon their return to Nevada, Sarah and Elma found things were worse than ever for their people. The settlers had taken more land from the Paiutes, and had formed an Indian shanty-town below C Street in Virginia City. The women would creep out before dawn to gather the refuse the white people had thrown away. They were happy to find half-rotten fruit or vegetables and bits of leftover meat. Once in a while a kind family would give them a bag of wheat. Sarah, too, was forced to go from home to home selling the needlework she had learned to make at the convent. Most of the money she earned went for books to fill her insatiable desire for knowledge. She knew an education was the key that would unlock the doors of repression and eventually set her people free.

Things appeared to improve for the Paiutes when President Lincoln appointed James Nye as governor of the Nevada Territory. Chief Winnemucca, in full Indian splendor and accompanied by select members of his tribe, went out to meet the new governor and escort him to their camp at Pyramid Lake. The officials were provided the hospitality of the tribe, but although the governor was quite impressed with the Paiutes, he did nothing to help their cause. The white men wanted all Indians to live on reservations while the size of the land allotted the Native Americans was decreasing. The settlers believed that any Indian who was not on a reservation was planning an uprising. Paiutes who attempted to pursue their hunting-and-gathering existence were disdainfully regarded as "diggers."

Chief Winnemucca had been approached by other tribes to join them in a fight for their rights, but he remained true to his peaceful beliefs. Because of this, he was forced to walk a thin line between the white men and the hostile Indians. The chief returned to the reservation that had been established at Pyramid Lake; it was no longer safe to roam the countryside.

By now Sarah Winnemucca had become a beautiful, outspoken woman who could read, write, and speak English fluently. She traveled from one reservation to another attempting to solve the Indians' problems. Her mother and older sister were dead. Elma had married a white rancher and moved to Montana. Sarah continued to work for her people, speaking to the American public and writing letters to Washington.

In 1870, when Sarah was 26, a reporter from the *Alta California* interviewed her in the town of Winnemucca, Nevada. He found her to be very well-informed and comely in appearance. She was able to converse freely about the condition of her people and their future prospects. In his column the reporter claimed Sarah had said to him, *... I am glad to see you, although I have no parlor to ask you into except the one made by nature for us all. I like the Indian life tolerable (sic) well, however, my only object in staying with these people is that I may do them good. I would rather be with my people, but not to live as they live. I was not raised so ...* [1] Sarah clearly preferred to live as a white woman, in a home, not wandering the desert. She was of two worlds. It was difficult to live in both and even more difficult to find a husband. Most Indians were uneducated, and although she was desired by many white men, none had shown any desire to wed.

All of that changed in 1871 when Sarah was 27 and the dashing, young Lieutenant Edward Bartlett noticed her sparkling personality and dark, flashing eyes. He was a fine horseman who admired the way Sarah rode her mount with ease. He appreciated her intelligence and rare Indian beauty. Later that year the couple were united in a simple ceremony in Salt Lake City, Utah.

Unfortunately, the marriage was a mistake for Sarah. Bartlett turned out to be a drunkard instead of the responsible man with whom she thought she had fallen in love. Within a few weeks he managed to drink his way through her small savings and sell what modest jewelry Sarah possessed. At that time Chief Winnemucca was living at Fort McDermit on the Oregon border. When he found out about the marriage, he came roaring down from the mountains like a wounded lion. Winnemucca did not believe in interracial marriages, and he claimed Sarah had dishonored the Paiutes. Natchez was sent to bring the misguided Princess back to her family, and Sarah willingly left her husband. She divorced Bartlett a few months later.

At Fort McDermit, Sarah began working as an interpreter for the Bureau of Indian Affairs. She dressed as a white woman in tailored suits and enjoyed the luxury of her own room. It was a happy period in her life. The commanding officer, Major Dudley Stewart, was a just man who wanted what was right for everyone.

---

1 A correspondent of **The Sacramento Record**, writing from Winnemucca, Nevada, for the **Alta California**, San Francisco. August 29, 1870, Bancroft Scraps, Vol. 93, p. 54.

Unfortunately, this was not to last. President Grant changed the prevailing laws, allowing no more treaties with the Indians. He declared the Indian people were wards of the government and as such were required to live on the reservations. Sarah fought back the only way she knew how— with words. Some of the Paiutes wanted a battle. Many fled to the surrounding hills, and all were starving.

Sarah moved to a new reservation at Malheur, Nevada, where she became an interpreter for Bureau of Indian Affairs Agent Sam Parrish, a fine, understanding man. Her people soon joined her. Parrish claimed the reservation belonged to the Indians, and he opened a school for the children. Under his guidance the Paiutes received individual plots of land and learned to dig irrigation ditches, cut rails for fences, and plant their own crops. Once more this was too good to last. Parrish was replaced by Agent Reinhard, who immediately reclaimed the plots of land and closed the Indian school. Reinhard was a bad example of an Indian agent, for he was as cruel as the system.

At first Sarah attempted to reason with Reinhard and offered to be of assistance. When that failed, she wrote a full report to Washington. Reinhard fired her and ordered the Princess off the reservation, threatening to put her in prison for being a trouble-maker. With their spokeswoman gone, the Paiutes faced more difficulties; and the majority blamed Sarah. Disease was rampant. They were cold and hungry, and many starved to death.

A Paiute messenger was sent to Sarah, who was working at a private home, to beg his Princess to use her gift of education and go to Washington. He asked her to speak to the "Great White Chief" on behalf of her people. The messenger further said the Paiutes were sorry to have lost faith in their "mother." Sarah took what few dollars she had saved and headed for Elko, Nevada, to raise funds for a trip to visit the President.

The Bannock War of 1878 temporarily ended her travels when Sarah was stopped by U.S. troops. They told her the Bannock Indians had captured her father and several other Paiutes because of their assistance to white men. Sarah joined the troops and accepted the responsibility of helping her people to escape from the hostile Indian camp. She went bravely through the Bannock lines disguised as a Bannock squaw and safely led the Paiutes out. At that time Chief Winnemucca declared she was more than a Paiute Princess, she was now their Queen.

Sarah remained with the army for the rest of the war, serving as a scout, helping with the injured and acting as an interpreter. She was a valuable asset to the troops because she knew the land well and could read the Bannock war signals, predicting what they were planning. Her unpleasant reward from the United States government came when the Paiutes were ordered as prisoners of war to the Yakima Reservation in the Washington Territory.

Stunned by the bad news, Sarah protested, claiming her people had always befriended the settlers and were not criminals. The order was not rescinded. In January 1879 a caravan of Paiutes set out for Yakima. The Indians were expected at the Malheur Reservation where there was food but instead were sent to Yakima to starve. Babies and old people died in route, and when the Paiutes arrived they were destitute. The agent, Father James Wilbur, put them in unprotected sheds without protection from the freezing weather.

Sarah and Natchez would not accept any more mistreatment of their people. They went to San Francisco to tell the citizens of that city about the plight of the Paiute. While there, Sarah appeared self-possessed before her audiences and she carried herself with dignity. Her eloquent speeches and fame in the Bannock War made her a celebrity. In 1879 the *San Francisco Chronicle* wrote: *"Sarah has undergone hardships and dared dangers that few men would be willing to face, but she never lost her womanly qualities ... She speaks with force and decision, and talks eloquently of her people. Her main mission, undertaken at the request of Chief Winnemucca, is to have her tribe gathered again at their old home in Nevada, where they can follow peaceable pursuits and improve themselves. ..."* [1]

Agent Reinhard countered her popularity by stating that Sarah was a liar and a "low" woman of questionable virtue. His accusations did not hinder Sarah; they inflamed her, and with the encouragement of many friends she continued to speak to capacity audiences

---

1 **San Francisco Chronicle,** November 17, 1879, California State Library.

about the ill treatment of the Paiutes.

Sarah made a striking picture in her bright red leggings and short buckskin dress bordered with colored fringe. Above her flowing dark hair she proudly wore a headdress of eagle feathers set in a scarlet crown. Sarah's voice rang out strong and clear, and the people believed her. While in San Francisco, she circulated a petition on behalf of the Paiutes, requesting that humane army officers instead of evil Indian agents handle their affairs. Sarah received so much acclaim that a special agent was sent from Washington to investigate the treatment of her people, and the Winnemucca family was invited to visit Washington to voice their complaints. Chief Winnemucca, Natchez, and Sarah left immediately for the Capitol on the Central Pacific Railroad. They were a proud, optimistic family.

Meanwhile, in order to protect himself, Agent Reinhard sent another letter to Washington that repeated his previous claims against Sarah. This time he added that she had been married several times, was an adulterous, an alcoholic, and a notorious liar. Then he obtained the signatures of three white men on an affidavit declaring he had written the truth. When the Department of the Interior received the letter, Sarah had little hope of achieving her goal.

The family arrived in Washington unaware the letter had been sent and received. The Winnemuccas wondered why they were surrounded by security and not allowed to converse with anyone. The department was afraid to let Sarah speak out against its agents, and the Paiute delegation was confined to a strict schedule. No reporters were allowed near the Winnemuccas. Finally, Sarah told her captors that she would have her say no matter what happened. When Secretary of the Interior Carl Schurz, found how determined she was, he promised the department would grant her wishes by letting the Paiutes return safely to the Malheur Reservation in Nevada. He further said he would send 100 tents and food for the people if she would leave Washington quietly. All of this was put on an official document signed by Schurz.

Before the Winnemuccas left Washington, they were granted a brief meeting with President Hayes, who asked Sarah if she had received what she came for. Sarah replied, "I think so," and the trusting delegation returned home to share the good news with their people. Sarah would not let the precious piece of paper with the written promises out of her sight. She guarded it with her life.

At the allotted time, Sarah and Natchez went to Lovelock, Nevada, where the tents and food were to arrive. They waited two weeks, and no tents appeared. The Indians who lived there started laughing at Sarah; they said she was a foolish woman to have trusted the white men. In desperation, Sarah wired Schurz, requesting his promise be fulfilled. He told her to go to Yakima with the document and bring her people home. This would mean a 300-mile trip for the starving Indians.

When Sarah arrived at Yakima and showed the document from the Department of the Interior to the agent, Father Wilbur, he refused to accept its contents. Wilbur told Sarah he would employ her as an interpreter if she would keep quiet about the document. He did not want the Paiutes to return to Nevada, claiming they were his best workers. Sarah turned the offer down and went to her people to explain what had happened, but they thought she was a traitor. She was humiliated and ashamed. Like her grandfather, she had believed the lies of the white men, and the Paiutes would suffer for her mistake. Some of the Indians tried to escape Yakima only to be captured and returned to the reservation. Most of the Paiutes accepted their fate and cried because they knew they would never see their land again.

Father Wilbur sent a letter to Schurz, claiming Sarah had misrepresented the Paiutes who were happy at Yakima. Then he banned Sarah from the reservation with no money and no place to go. She contacted an old friend, General Howard, who sent for her to teach the children of the Bannock prisoners at Vancouver Barracks. Sarah had been betrayed by the whites and now was despised by her own race; they thought she had sold them out for her own material gains. Before she left Yakima, Sarah told Father Wilbur that she believed Hell must be full of Christians like him.

In 1881, at the age of 37, Sarah met her second husband, Lewis Hopkins, a white man who was several years younger than she. This time the Princess picked a gambling man, and within a few weeks he had lost all the money she had earned while teaching at Vancouver. He was unemployed and preferred to remain that way. Once more Sarah had to return to the Indian way of life. The couple left for Pyramid Lake Reservation, and when they arrived found the Indians working the land and the agent reaping the harvest. Everything went into his pocket.

Sarah was tired of false promises and conditions forcing the Paiutes to starve. She again decided to take her case before the American people and in 1883, when Sarah was 39, she and Hopkins left Nevada for a lecture tour of the East Coast. They had very little money and needed many friends. In Boston, Sarah found the friends when she met two influential sisters, Elizabeth Peabody and Mary Mann, the widow of educator Horace Mann. These women were so impressed with Sarah's impassioned plea for her people that they wholeheartedly supported her cause. Both sisters assisted Sarah in her lectures and encouraged her to write a book which they promised to publish.

With these two women firmly behind her, Princess Sarah traveled throughout the East for several months pleading for the freedom of her people. Once again she created a colorful impression dressed in fringed buckskins and beads, wearing a golden crown and carrying a red velvet wampum bag. A few newspapers carried stories claiming Sarah was an unscrupulous and unreliable woman who was really a camp-follower. Others said it was the Indian Bureau — not Sarah Winnemucca — that was offensive. Hundreds of people came forward to defend the dramatic Princess' honor and participate in her cause. She was even endorsed by the Boston Friends of Peace, and her autobiography was published. Sarah Winnemucca was the first Indian woman to write a book.

The sisters continued to give freely, and thousands of people turned out to hear Sarah speak. Her husband would first appear on stage to introduce Sarah and tell of her past. Then the Princess would come forward in her native costume. Since she spoke from her heart, the people believed her. Following the lecture Sarah would sign copies of her book, *Life Among the Paiutes*. A petition was circulated requesting that the Indians be given lands and citizens' rights. It was signed by 5,000 people, and representatives prepared to present legislation in the House.

For the first time, everything seemed to be going Sarah's way. Then however, her husband became unhappy with their financial arrangements. Sarah's work was for her people, and the money collected from the lectures and book sales was to go toward a school for Paiute children. Hopkins wanted to spend it on fancy clothing and gambling debts. When the series of lectures was over, Sarah went to take the money out of the bank and found most of it had already been withdrawn. The account was in both Sarah's and Hopkins' names, so no explanation was necessary. He had taken her hard-earned savings.

With a heavy heart and an empty purse, Sarah returned to Nevada. Her work had been in vain. The money was gone, and most of the people soon forgot her cause — the Legislature did nothing to help the Paiutes. All Sarah had to show for her efforts were a few barrels of old clothing that had been collected for the families of her tribe. Sarah had lost her battle and was resented by her own people. Hopkins was diagnosed as having tuberculosis, and the couple returned to the reservation at Pyramid Lake.

Meanwhile, Senator Leland Stanford, founder of Stanford University in California, became interested in the Indians' problems and Sarah's devotion to her people caught his attention. He gave Sarah and Natchez 160 acres of land near Lovelock, Nevada, and at last Sarah was able to start a school while Natchez farmed the land. The school was called "Peabody's Institute," and it was a place where Indians could learn.

Sarah used the Bible as a textbook, and the students sang gospel hymns. In order to help the youngsters remain in class while their families were hunting and gathering, Sarah, with Elizabeth Peabody's assistance, turned the school into a boarding home. The children were able to learn housework and farming as well as academic studies. Sarah took no money for herself; the school was her reward. She was doing what she had always dreamed of, and the children were superior students. Sarah wanted them to learn well and become teachers who would go forward and educate their own race.

Sarah Winnemucca's work, however, was to again end in

failure. The white settlers were resentful because Natchez, an Indian, owned land and Sarah's students were receiving a better education than their own. The envious neighbors cut off the water supply to the farm, and the school closed. It reopened temporarily, with Elizabeth Peabody's help and donations from kind people in the East. Sarah was able to keep it going for another year until the death of her husband. She had learned to love Hopkins despite his faults, and her heart was broken.

Following Hopkins' funeral, the discouraged Sarah, who had lost not only her husband but her faith in the white people as well, returned to the tribe where she lived as an Indian. When her health began to fail in 1890, Sarah moved to Montana to spend her last few months with her sister Elma. On October 17, 1891, Princess Sarah Winnemucca died of tuberculosis contracted from her husband. She was 47 years old.

Sarah had led a dedicated life, fought a long and fruitless battle, and earned the respect of a nation. Because of her, the Paiutes began to think and work for their own rights. Today the tribe is moving ahead, looking towards the future, and respectfully looking over its shoulder at the vision of a Paiute Princess named Sarah, who will always be remembered as their own personal "Indian Joan of Arc."

THE PRINCESS' LECTURE

Sarah Winnemucca lectured at Metropolitan Hall, San Francisco, Tuesday evening, on "the Manners and Customs of Indian Women." Chief Natchez and five or six Piutes (sic) sat upon the platform, all decked out with plumes and beads. The Indian Princess made an earnest appeal for homes and land that her race may call their own, and gave a description of the present condition of the Piutes. Chief Natchez made a few remarks, which were translated by his sister.

In the afternoon she gave a lecture at the same place to women. She began with a description of the customs of her people forty years ago. She told how, in the Summer, the women remained at home gathering roots and herbs while the young men returned home and all the tribes assembled in their villages. Then the sounds of merriment rose from the wigwams. There were games, and songs and dances, and at night, in their own language, they prayed to the Great Spirit to keep them from disease and make them good. In the wigwam the grandmother is the guardian of the young girls. Never can they speak with any man who is not a near relative, father or brother. With the Indians there is no walking or riding with the young men and boys, "as is common with your daughters, my white sister," said the Princess. The girls remain at home. But when she is no longer a child, but a woman, she is treated like a queen.

The children are to a great extent self-taught. The boys are present when the chiefs meet in council and when the debate is over they go out on some hillside and act it all over. They choose and name their chiefs and talk as they heard their fathers talk. The girls too, in their games, imitate the labors of their elders, and at evening they gather around their grandmother and she tells them Indian legends and traditions, pausing once in a while to say, "You would not have done so," and the eager little ones cry, "No, no." Or she says, "You will all be brave like this," and the chorus answers, "Yes." So they learn the history of their tribe. "But," said the Princess, "this was all before my people became civilized, before the white men came among us and brought us cards and whisky (sic), and taught us to drink and lie and smoke."

She answered in behalf of her people, if they must have civilization, give them the highest type; give them the ballot so they can stand on a par with the colored race, and give them deeds of their lands and schools to educate them in the English language.

Reese River Reveille, February 13, 1885
Courtesy of The Nevada Historical Society

Note: Paiute is spelled Piute in this column. Both spellings are correct.

Sarah Winnemucca during her visit to San Francisco

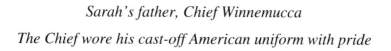

Sarah's father, Chief Winnemucca

The Chief wore his cast-off American uniform with pride

◆ ──────────────────────────────── ◆

*Sarah Winnemucca on her Eastern tour pleading
for her people's rights*

Fanny Stenhouse

Chapter 4

FANNY STENHOUSE & ANN ELIZA YOUNG
The Tyranny of Polygamy

A uthor's note: This story is about two fascinating women who were caught up in the web of polygamy. It is meant to entertain, not to cast slurs upon the Mormon faith, as the author is neither pro-Mormon nor anti-Mormon. Since most of the information in this chapter has been taken from Fanny Stenhouse's autobiography, reprinted in 1888, its accuracy cannot be proven. However, further research into the subject substantiates almost all of the statements as they are presented. The fact that plural wives were viewed as mere property of their husbands and were often referred to as "cows" is shown in more than one of the books about polygamy. One Christian worker summarized the situation of plural marriage by writing in the Chicago Advance, "Nearly all the Mormons believed in polygamy but less than one-fourth practiced it; moreover, if the women were left to themselves, nine-tenths of them would vote it so thoroughly out of existence that it would never be heard from again." [1]

Fanny Stenhouse was born in 1829 on an island in the English channel and was raised as a member of the Baptist Church. She was introduced to Mormonism while a young woman, when she met and fell in love with her future husband, Elder Thomas Stenhouse. He was a penniless religious man who was filled with more than the usual amount of missionary zeal. Stenhouse spent a great deal of his time spreading the gospel and seeking converts to enter the Church of Jesus Christ of Latter-Day Saints. Because of her love for Thomas, Fanny agreed to leave her own religion and was baptized into the Mormon faith.

1 **The Woman's Movement 1869-1896**, by Beverly Benton

Within a few months the couple were wed, and Fanny cast aside all her former ties to cling to her husband, helping him in his work. In Europe at that time, polygamy was only a whisper that Elder Stenhouse dismissed as idle gossip. This gossip, however, became fact in 1852, when Fanny was 23 years old and the mother of two. Joseph Smith, the Prophet and founder of the Mormon Church, had a revelation regarding "celestial marriage" in 1843, but the "revelation" was not announced until 1852, nine years later. In his document, Smith declared that polygamy was commanded by God and that it was a sacred order to be followed by the righteous. The doctrine of celestial marriage was set down by Prophet Smith, and Brigham Young later added several of his own beliefs. These were recorded in Fanny Stenhouse's autobiography *"The Tyranny of Mormonism"* and Kimball Young's *"Isn't One Wife Enough."* A few of the teachings that are important to this chapter follow:

A Latter-Day Saint would faithfully marry more than one wife under the celestial marriage system for time and eternity so that *he* might advance to a god in *his* own world and a king in the hereafter. It was believed that the more children brought forth, the more spirits would enter the world and embrace Mormonism. There were three different types of marriages. The first, secular, was for "time" only, with the bonds of matrimony severed at the death of either spouse or any Mormon who was not "sealed," or acknowledged in the proper manner, by the Church. The second form of marriage was for "time" and "eternity." Such marriages bound a man and his wives for all eternity. The third form was for "eternity" only. This was to accommodate the men whose wives had died before they were sealed, entitling them to be reunited in heaven. It was a ritual that was performed by proxy, with the second wife as a "stand-in" for the first wife.

The Church believed it was better to have multiple wives rather than to participate in adultery like many Gentiles. The doctrine of Trinity taught the faithful that in order to attain the pinnacle of glory in the next world there must be at least three wives, thus adding more jewels to their crowns in the hereafter. Although plural marriage was not legitimate in the eyes of the law, it was recognized by the Mormon Church. Polyandry (the taking of multiple husbands by a woman) was not allowed, for one woman could not bring forth the quota of children to fulfill the "Grand Design."

This was the strange life that awaited Fanny Stenhouse and her children. At first she was filled with alarm, then a terror that could only be calmed by her husband's promise that they would live a monogamous life. During the early years of his marriage to Fanny, Thomas Stenhouse had done more than preach the gospel. He had become the successful editor of a leading London newspaper. Following the announcement of the new doctrine, it was only natural that he would be "called" by Brigham Young to move to Zion (Salt Lake City) to further spread the word throughout the new land.

Fanny and her children were expected to leave their comfortable home behind and put their lives in the hands of the Church. In 1856 the family set sail for the "Promised Land." When the ship left England, Fanny had a heavy heart and carried a new baby in her arms. Following a long and difficult voyage, they arrived in New York, only to find they were to participate in one of the many "Handcart" migrations across the plains to Zion. The rigors and tragedy of previous handcart expeditions had been described to Fanny by her friend Mary, who had been on one of the first migrations. Mary had written of the thousands of men, women and children who traveled across the prairies and mountains for 1,300 miles, pulling their worldly possessions in handmade, two-wheel carts. They had little shelter and hardly any food, and many people froze to death. Remembering her friend's letter, Fanny was terrified about the trip that lay ahead. But the Stenhouses had no choice; they had to obey the Church.

When the family finally arrived safely in Salt Lake after their long difficult journey, they were provided with a humble dwelling in which to live. Although the Stenhouses were used to finer quarters, they considered themselves lucky, as many people were living in tents. Fanny was eager to see the City of the Saints and to meet the residents. What she found both surprised and shocked her. Some families were living in hovels, others in mansions. One poor woman was as pale as death and seemed very unhappy. She told Fanny that her husband was marrying a girl of 14, and showed Fanny the miserable hut where they were all to live. Another lady she regarded with particular interest was Eliza R. Snow, one of the Prophet Smith's wives. Eliza had been the first woman married in polygamy after Joseph Smith received the revelation. Her principle occupation was converting rebellious wives to obedience to their husbands and convincing young girls that it was their duty to enter into polygamy. She was considered by many to be a fanatic who counseled unhappy husbands and acted as the "Representative of Eve" in the mysteries of the Endowment House, where the religious ceremonies were conducted.

Fanny also met "Aunty Shearer," a tall, angular woman with pale, unhappy eyes. It was said that Mrs. Shearer was an early disciple who sacrificed everything for Mormonism and was instructed by the "immaculate Joseph" in the ways of polygamy. He taught her to overcome her feelings and convinced her to be married to him for eternity. Poor and forgotten, a relic of a woman who was once one of the Prophet's spiritual wives, she lived in a lonely hut when Fanny met her.

Since Fanny and Thomas Stenhouse had not been properly sealed, they were not wed in the eyes of the Church. *"We were told that we had never been married at all, and that our husbands and children were not lawfully ours ... for a marriage to be valid it must be solemnized in the Endowment House in Salt Lake City, or persons can never be expected to be husband and wife in eternity."* Fanny also described spiritual wives, saying, *"Spiritual wives are of two kinds, the one consists of old ladies who have plenty of money or property, which of course needs looking after; and the generous elders marry them, and accordingly (look after) the said property, and the owner of the property becomes a spiritual wife and will only be his wife in eternity when she is rejuvenated. ...The other kind of spiritual wife, or one who is sealed to the Brethren, who is better able to exalt her, shall pass from he who is her husband on earth to him who is to be her husband in heaven."*

All of this was confusing and upsetting to Fanny and left her with a feeling of outrage. She saw families consisting of husbands with several wives living in poverty while the men looked around for younger wives. One man had married two women on the same day, and both wives dressed exactly alike so that neither could claim precedence of the other. In many cases a man would marry two sisters or a mother and her daughter. Fanny resented the fact that the man was considered to be the head and "saviour" of the woman, and that the woman was only responsible to her husband. If the woman disobeyed, she would not enter heaven as a queen; she would only be an angel. She also thought it was ridiculous to believe a woman who neither married or was given in marriage would serve as a slave to the "Saints" in the hereafter. Fanny was totally disenchanted with Mormonism and was glad she was not a polygamous wife, for the Elder Stenhouse was still true to his word.

Shortly after the Stenhouses' arrival in Salt Lake City, they visited President Young and were graciously received. Fanny was impressed and relieved by his affable manner and the fact that his wives seemed to be happy, kind-hearted women. At that time Brigham Young was a handsome, well-built man with an air of one who was used to being obeyed. Fanny knew he had many wives, and she noticed that Brigham and the rest of the brethren often sought wives with qualities which would help in their business or the running of their homes. Each wife would be chosen to serve in a different capacity, creating a smooth way of life. There were cooks, laundresses, hostesses and mothers, all profitable to the husband. It was less expensive to marry a woman than to hire her for wages. Many of the wives were ignored or neglected, and others would become reigning favorites for a period of time. The first wife was treated with respect and often called "mother" by the other wives. Some of Brigham Young's wives were spiritual and three of the older women had been married to the Prophet Joseph Smith. They had been sealed to Brigham following the Prophet's death and would rejoin him in heaven.

As Fanny visited with the other wives she saw the devastating results of polygamy in their homes. Several of the wives could not accept the humiliation of their husbands' continuous courting of younger women. Fanny hated seeing the women slaving for their husbands' glory and exaltation in the world to come. The sight of children miserably clad, barefoot, gaunt and hungry haunted Fanny as much as the sight of children of wealthy fathers who ignored them to chase after new, younger wives. On the other hand, she saw many women who were full of religious zeal and who encouraged their husbands to take multiple wives. These women accepted the doctrines of the Church, believing it was their duty to minister to the men and the men, in return, would save them in the kingdom of heaven if they behaved themselves.

According to Mormon beliefs of the day, the first wife was supposed to have the right to decide upon a polygamous marriage. If she refused, the marriage could not take place. This, however, was not upheld. Fanny wrote, *"If the first wife refused, there were other ways she could be coerced into acceptance, including her own death."* The prophet was also known to arrange or "suggest" multiple marriages among his elders, and they did not dare refuse. This is what happened to the Stenhouses.

Fanny realized her husband was acting strangely, and she anticipated he was about to break his promise to her and end their monogamous marriage. She knew he was a good Mormon and it was inevitable. When he finally told her he was adding another wife to their household, Fanny became rebellious, refusing to allow the marriage. Members of the Church, including Eliza Snow, spent hours working with Fanny. They convinced her that she had no choice in the matter. Fanny, in order to save face, was allowed the privilege of selecting the new wife. This custom was often practiced. It made the husband happy and eased his conscience because, after all, the first wife had picked the second one. Usually the new wife had already been chosen; it was just a polite process they went through.

In Fanny's case it was especially hard, as the second wife was merely a pretty girl. Fanny was consumed with sadness for she had passed her prime and was forced to watch her husband woo a younger woman. Fanny steeled herself to accept, but the sight of her Thomas courting the girl was almost too much for her to bear; she felt that somehow she had lost her own identity.

The next ordeal Fanny had to suffer was the most painful that any loving wife and mother could endure. She had to give her husband to another wife — for that was the sacrifice demanded of Mormon women during the reign of polygamy. Fanny was filled with dread and forebodings as she knelt before the alter in the Endowment House to place the hand of the new wife into that of her husband's. When she left the ceremony, Fanny was not the same. There were now two Mrs. Stenhouses. Life lost its charm, and in her misery Fanny completely gave up her husband. Divorce was out of the question for although he had deserted her, she still loved her husband. Fanny would wait and watch, and she knew someday the Elder Stenhouse would learn for himself the heartache and deception of a polygamous life.

It was several years before Thomas Stenhouse began to see the folly of multiple marriage and of the Church. His love life was not to provide the rewarding experience he expected. Following his first venture into polygamy, he began to court a third younger wife. It was then his second wife who endured the misery and sorrow of stepping aside for another. Fanny had no feelings one way or the other. As far as she was concerned Thomas already had one wife too many, so what difference would one more or even 100 more make. It was the second wife who was unhappy as she realized she was no longer the elder's young love. This wife, however, was not like Fanny; another woman in the house was not for her. Within a few weeks she went to Brigham Young, complaining that she led a miserable life and was not happy with the Elder Stenhouse. When the prophet heard her sad tale, he provided the woman with a $10 divorce and set her free. Meanwhile, the bride-to-be decided to marry a handsome, wealthier man, leaving Thomas back where he had started, with one wife.

The number of Mormons becoming disenchanted with celestial marriage was on the rise, and plural marriages were declining. Thomas Stenhouse often had to travel on business and, out in the world away from Salt Lake City, he soon began to doubt his own faith. Mormonism had been everything to him for most of his adult life. Now he felt betrayed, not by the loss of his bride-elect or by the loss of his second wife but by the Church itself. Thomas, had looked around and he could no longer believe. After agonizing over the situation for months, he sent a letter to Bishop Young to renounce his claim to the "Infallible Priesthood," and he sold his newspaper.

Released at last from polygamy, Fanny took her rightful place beside her husband. The couple's children had grown into adulthood, and they had cut themselves off from their past associations and friendships. The Stenhouses were considered unbelievers, or apostates, in the eyes of the Church.

With the world before them, the Stenhouses left Salt Lake City and moved to New York, where Thomas again started his own newspaper. Although he no longer believed in Mormonism, he could not become its opponent. When he wrote about the Latter-Day Saints, it was to remind people that no one man can set himself up as God. Thomas declared not even the Prophet has the right to decide the destiny of the thousands of decent Mormons who are honorable, God-fearing people.

Fanny began a series of lecture tours describing her life in polygamy. She encouraged all women to stand up for themselves, for she was sure each person had the right to earn her own place in heaven. Later she wrote articles and in 1874 completed her auto-biography. While Fanny was doing all this, a new voice began to ring out throughout the land. It was that of Ann Eliza Webb Young, the woman who was brave enough to divorce Brigham Young and whose crusade against polygamy helped to bring the pillars of celestial marriage tumbling down.

Ann Eliza was the antithesis of the patient Fanny Stenhouse. She was a beautiful, outspoken woman who first accepted Brigham Young and his "harem," then started a campaign that would blow the prophet and polygamy to shreds.

She was born on September 3, 1844, in Nauvoo, Illinois, to Eliza and Chauncey Webb. At that time there were four children in the Webb family: Ann Eliza and her three brothers. Unlike Fanny, she was raised a Mormon. Her mother was a quiet woman who taught school and had a fanatical love of the Church. Ann Eliza's father was a successful carriage maker and a practicing polygamist. He had taken his first wife in polygamy when Ann Eliza was 3 years old, and by the time she was 12 he had added three more.

In 1846 most Americans despised polygamy, and anti-Mormon sentiment in Nauvoo began increasing. To escape the danger,

Ann Eliza Webb Young

Chauncey packed up his belongings and with his family joined a group of Saints heading West. They first located in a Mormon settlement in Missouri, where Webb temporarily opened a carriage shop. He knew the family would be called to Salt Lake City soon, and he wanted to set aside supplies and money for the long journey. Chauncey was a fine craftsman and the Webbs were prosperous. When they finally left for Salt Lake, they traveled in style. Ann Eliza had grown into a precocious 4-year-old. At that time Chauncey had two wives.

Following their arrival, Chauncey again opened a carriage shop and continued to support his growing family with an above average income. He added three more wives to his harem and built a large farmhouse where they all lived quietly. But all was not as it appeared. As Ann Eliza grew into her teens, she began to notice her mother's increasing resentment toward the other wives. Competition was high; and although the women tried to get along, it was really their religion that kept them together. Ann Eliza also saw how hard it was for her father, as he tried to treat all the women equally. She once commented that under the circumstances he did remarkably well, and he never referred to his wives as "cows," like many of the other Mormon men did.

Growing into maturity with her own mother and four women she called "mother" was very difficult for Ann Eliza, and it had a negative effect upon her own marriages. She did not like polygamy and although she had been baptized a Mormon, Ann Eliza vowed she would never become a plural wife. Brigham Young, however, had other plans for the lovely girl. When she first caught his attention, she was 17 and on the arm of one of her many suitors. The prophet realized that little Ann Eliza had grown into a beautiful young woman.

Brigham immediately went to her mother and ordered Eliza Webb to break up her daughter's affairs with other men. The overly religious Eliza promptly obeyed. Then, although Ann Eliza had no previous acting experience, Brigham invited her to join his theatrical group. When the young woman agreed, the 61-year-old prophet began to court her. At that time he already had many wives and was known to have once married 11 women within a period of

23 days. Ann Eliza, though, had been wooed before. By the time she was 12, she had already received 10 proposals from leading Saints. It would seem that the Mormon elders of that era liked their women young.

Despite his efforts, the aging prophet was not to be Ann Eliza's first husband. She lost her heart to a young actor, James Dee, who she married against her mother's wishes. The couple were sealed in the Endowment House by an unsmiling Brigham Young. Dee, also a Mormon, promised his young bride she would be his only wife, but within a few months he was chasing other women. Throughout the following three years, Ann Eliza bore Dee two sons and endured his physical abuse. When she could no longer bear the mistreatment, Ann Eliza returned to her father's home for refuge. A few months later, with the help of Brigham Young, she divorced her husband and settled down to raise her children alone.

During the subsequent year, Ann Eliza regained her natural sparkle and charm. She had many suitors and proposals of marriage, but she rejected them, claiming her children were her only loves. Ann Eliza remained a divorcee and lived quietly until Brigham Young again entered her life. Accompanied by marching bands and a large entourage, he paid a visit to the small community in which the Webbs lived to attend a prayer meeting. The prophet seemed to have grown in stature since Ann Eliza had last seen him. She was just a girl at that time. Having matured to a woman, she recognized him as a dominant figure, one that she could no longer ignore. Her femininity and beauty were even more desirable to Brigham Young than before, and he knew he was to wed Ann Eliza.

He first requested Ann Eliza's hand in marriage from her parents, who immediately gave their consent. They thought it was a great honor for their daughter to receive such a fine offer from their religious leader. Ann Eliza, however, was shocked and frightened. Although she realized his power, she wanted nothing to do with a man of his age who already had more women and children than he could possibly care for. Undefeated, Brigham told the young woman he would be her protector and a father to her children. When she refused, he said it was her duty. Prophet Young's constant attention and her parents' pleas and tears finally wore Ann Eliza down. In 1869, at the age of 24, she became the last and most difficult wife of the 68-year-old prophet.

Following their marriage, Brigham was reluctant to take his new bride home. He feared the wrath of Amelia, the reigning favorite, and the disapproval of the rest of his wives. Ann Eliza spent her wedding night at her parents' home. The prophet, however, was quite attentive and visited his new wife nightly, eventually moving her into a residence of her own. Most of Brigham's wives lived at the Lion House, but for special women he kept other homes throughout the city. In addition, he had the Bee Hive House, where he lived with the reigning favorite, and the Farmhouse which provided all of the dairy products for his large family.

The house he placed Ann Eliza into was less than she had expected. She had been promised a life of luxury and comfort but was given a small, shabbily furnished place with a used carpet on the floor, cast-off furniture and broken dishes. For one who had been so royally sought-after, it was almost a physical blow. Things became worse when third-rate food was delivered to her home, and Brigham provided insufficient financial support. Ann Eliza was totally disenchanted. She had planned to replace Amelia as Brigham Young's favorite, but she was mistaken. Once he possessed Ann Eliza, she became just another fancy jewel that he added to his crown. Amelia still ruled his harem, outside of Young's occasional visit to one of his wives.

Ann Eliza and her sons soon began visiting the Lion House for meals and prayer. The food, although plain, was nourishing; and she enjoyed the company of the other women. Her first visit was strained as most of the wives looked upon her youth and beauty as a threat to their own well-being. The prophet ruled his house with a firm hand. Each woman had her own duties and place in his life. They were afraid that the uninvited newcomer would change their status and destroy their routine — Ann Eliza was a rival.

According to Fanny Stenhouse, Brigham Young had 19 wives, and Ann Eliza was his 15th, the rest being spiritual only. Irving Wallace, in his book *The Twenty-Seventh Wife,* claims there were 27, which is no doubt closer to the truth. Ann Eliza always considered herself Brigham's 19th wife. Wallace has done extensive research on both Brigham Young and Ann Eliza Webb. Fanny Stenhouse also wrote that many wives had died or strayed without being counted and *"no one cared."* Brigham Young's first known wife died before he became a Mormon convert. His first legal wife in the Church was Mary Ann Angell, who was described by Fanny Stenhouse as being *"a very fine-looking old lady and very much devoted to her unfaithful lord and master."* Mary Ann lived alone and, for the sake of appearances, Brigham would occasionally take her to a party. She had five children by the prophet and her oldest son would follow Brigham as president of the Church.

Wives number two and three were sisters Lucy and Clara Decker. Harriet Cook, wife number four, was a tall, light-haired, blue-eyed woman. She was no longer entitled to Brigham's affections because she had been disobedient. Lucy Bigelow was number five; and Mrs. Twiss, number six. Mrs. Twiss had no children and was given the dubious honor of being the housekeeper in the Bee Hive House.

Wife number seven was quiet and lived as a spinster; and Harriet Barney Seagers, the eighth, was another man's wife when Brigham made love to her. She believed the word of the prophet was the revelation of the Lord, and she lived a forgotten life, regretting her folly. Eliza Burgess, the ninth wife, asked Brigham to marry her. She was his only English bride and bore him one son. Susan Snively, number 10, was an industrious German woman who Brigham placed in the Farmhouse. She supplied the butter and cheese for his family, as well as for the marketplace. Margaret Pierce was number 11 and was a very unhappy woman.

Emmeline Free, number 12, was at one time the reigning favorite. She was described by Fanny as the most handsome of the wives, *"tall and graceful, with curling hair, beautiful eyes and complexion."* When Brigham left her bed for a younger woman, her sorrow almost caused her death. Emmeline was replaced by Amelia Folsom, his 13th wife and the one who remained his favorite until the day he died. Amelia resided in the Bee Hive House with the prophet, and he dressed her in the finest jewels and clothing money could buy. The rest of his wives wore wools and cottons. The wives bore Brigham Young 56 children. The last child

— borne by Mary Van Cott, his young 14th wife — arrived nine months after his marriage to Ann Eliza Webb.

Although so many wives were hard to accept, Ann Eliza soon became friends with most of them. Amelia, however, never recognized the "19th" wife. She had been the head of Brigham's harem for six years and planned to remain in that position. This was quite evident at all the social functions. Amelia was seated to the right of the prophet — a place of honor — during theatrical performances, and she always had the first dance with him at the balls. As custom demanded, Brigham would dance once with each of his wives, then return to dance the rest of the evening with Amelia.

In her book, Fanny Stenhouse described a ballroom scene, writing, *"These balls afford splendid opportunity to the men for flirting with the girls. No matter how old and homely a man is, he thinks he has as much right to flirt and dance with the girls as the youngest boy; for they all look upon themselves and each other as boys and single men, even if they have a dozen wives. There is no limit to their privileges. They are always in the market. Brigham, in his public discourses, has said that the brethren are all young men under a hundred years of age."*[1] It was no wonder the wives hated the ballroom dances.

As time passed, Ann Eliza saw less and less of Brigham Young. Although he had been an ardent lover at first, it was obvious that he was sharing his favors with his other wives, especially Amelia. The promises he made to help raise her sons were not fulfilled. The boys were not accepted, and they were given cast-off clothing to wear. As the prophet's visits grew fewer, her allowance decreased. Ann Eliza was forced to take boarders into her home to support herself and her sons. Most of these were Gentiles, or non-believers in the Mormon faith. These men recognized the plight of the poor woman and they sympathized with her.

During this period she met Major Pond, a reporter for the *Tribune*, and the Reverend C. C. Stratton, a Methodist minister, and his wife. Since she had no one to turn to, Ann Eliza found herself pouring her story out to these kind, understanding people. By that time she was so emotionally shattered that her appearance had begun to suffer. A few days after the talk with Pond and the

---

1 **The Tyranny of Mormonism**, by Fanny Stenhouse

Strattons, her old, worn-out wood stove fell apart; and when she asked Brigham for help, he ignored her. That was the last straw. Ann Eliza asked her boarders to leave, sent her older son to her parents, and requested the help of the Reverend Stratton and his wife.

At that point in her life, she hated Brigham Young, not the Church. The Strattons were understanding and suggested that she move out of her home to the protection of the local hotel which was owned by Gentiles. Ann Eliza agreed, and she turned what little decent furniture she had acquired over the years to the auctioneer. On July 15, 1875, six years after she married Brigham Young, she took her son and moved into the hotel. She decided to divorce the prophet and tell the people of the world of her treatment and that of other wives suffering the bondage of polygamy. All of this was done at great risk, for Ann Eliza knew her life and that of her son were in peril. Within the Church were men known as the Danites. They were masked avengers who would seek out and punish any Mormon caught speaking against the Church. She had openly defied the Latter-Day Saints and was divorcing the prophet. Ann Eliza was terrified.

When Brigham Young heard what his rebellious wife was doing, he was furious. But Ann Eliza had created such a national sensation that he would not dare touch her. Reporters from all the leading newspapers started arriving in Salt Lake City, seeking interviews with the defenseless wife. Ann Eliza, pale and worn, welcomed them one at a time into her room on the top floor of the hotel, where she had been placed for safety. She was very gracious; and when she told her moving story, she immediately won the reporters' support. Americans had been against polygamy for years, and they eagerly awaited her words.

Major Pond encouraged her to go on a lecture tour to expose the terrible injustices endured by the women of Utah. But Ann Eliza was still afraid to leave her room. She was divorcing Brigham Young for neglect and non-support, and she demanded a settlement of $200,000. Her name was in all the newspapers, and she was filled with apprehension. The Mormon men were filled with anger!

Two months after her self-imposed isolation, Ann Eliza, her son, and a woman companion slipped away from the hotel under cover of darkness. She kept looking over her shoulder in terror of the Danites, only relaxing when they were safely out of Utah.

Ann Eliza's first lecture was delivered in Denver, with Major Pond acting as her agent. Trembling but determined to let the world know what was happening, she spoke to a full house. When she finished, Ann Eliza was greeted with thunderous applause — she had been successful.

Brigham Young countered her accusations by calling Ann Eliza a cold, unloving woman who only sought his money. He further claimed their marriage was not valid, and he spread scandalous stories about her. At one time Brigham accused Ann Eliza of having an affair with Major Pond. This, however, was out of the question as she had always lived and traveled with a respectable female companion. When his slanderous remarks failed, Brigham reverted to religion, sending members of his Church to convince his erring wife to return home.

Ann Eliza would have none of it. She continued to lecture against polygamy and the prophet to well-attended audiences throughout the land. She spoke with dignity and strength. She was so forceful that while in Washington, Congress recessed to listen. Later, in 1882, her eloquent lectures helped to pass a federal bill banning polygamy in the territories. Ann Eliza also wrote her autobiography, *Wife No. 19* or *The Story of a Life in Bondage,* which became a best-seller.

Meanwhile, her parents were suffering. The Church had turned upon them; and her mother began to write tearful letters, begging Ann Eliza to reconsider and return to the fold. When her daughter sadly refused, Eliza Webb wrote that her death would have been preferable to the course she was taking. This broke Ann Eliza's heart, but there could be no turning back. She would continue her lectures and pursue her divorce. Brigham Young and celestial marriage had to end.

Ann Eliza was receiving unanimous acclaim from the press and speaking to standing-room only audiences. Requests for engagements poured in from all over the nation, as she described the lurid revelations of Joseph Smith. Eventually Ann Eliza's lectures became so moving that her mother began to see Brigham Young through her daughter's eyes, and Eliza Webb came to stand beside her. Eliza then shared her own struggle to maintain dignity while living within a plural marriage.

It took five years for the courts to settle the divorce. The final decision came in April 1877. After a long battle and many appeals, the court stated that although Ann Eliza and Brigham Young had lived together as man and wife, their marriage was not valid in the eyes of the government. She received a token of $3,600, and the case was closed. Ann Eliza was glad it was over. She had made thousands of dollars from her lectures and sales of her books. More importantly, she had told the world about polygamy.

Brigham Young died from an appendicitis attack September 2 1877. He was 76 years old. The prophet was laid to rest in a simple wooden box, and it was said that 40,000 mourners passed by his coffin before he was buried. Brigham's property was divided among his large family as he had directed, and each wife went on to fulfill her own destiny.

In 1883 Ann Eliza married her third husband, Moses R. Denning, a prominent, wealthy man from Michigan. Two years later, when Ann Eliza was 41, polygamy was coming to an end. In 1890 federal agents moved into the Utah Territory and the Church relinquished the practice of celestial marriage. Ann Eliza was 46 years old when she enjoyed the sweet feeling of victory. Her life, however, was not to have a happy ending. She and Denning separated in 1892, and a year later she divorced him for infidelity.

Following the divorce she lived alone, writing and occasionally lecturing. She later revised her book, *Wife No. 19,* but people had lost interest in the subject. No further history of Ann Eliza Webb Young is available, as she vanished from sight in 1908 at the age of 64.

For an interesting, detailed account of Ann Eliza Webb's story, the author highly recommends the book "The Twenty-Seventh Wife" by Irving Wallace.

Handcart Pioneers

THE HANDCART MIGRATION

From 1856 to 1860 thousands of Latter-Day Saints embarked upon one of the most remarkable journeys America has ever seen. Hundreds of men, women and children literally walked almost 1,300 miles to Zion. They came from all over the world, seeking freedom from oppression and ready to die for the glory of the Church — and many did. Their song, "Some Must Push and Some Must Pull," rang out over the mountains and prairies as these brave, dedicated people made their way to join Brigham Young in the green valley of Salt Lake City.

Most of the first expeditions were successful; but as more and more families clamored to make the trip, it became almost impossible to take them safely across the plains. The handcarts they used were hastily thrown together, constructed of unseasoned wood with little or no iron. There were 20 carts per hundred people, with five to a cart. Each person was allowed to carry 17 pounds of baggage, including their clothing, bedding, and utensils.

Five tents were provided for every hundred people; and stronger, heavier wagons pulled by oxen carried the provisions, which were rationed out. The food was inadequate, consisting of three-quarters of a pound of flour a day, with three ounces of sugar and a half-pound of bacon a week. As the expedition progressed, even that small amount of nourishment decreased. Children cried from hunger, and the men had barely enough strength to pull the flimsy carts, with many fainting to the ground. Starving women nursed their babies as they plodded along.

*In her book, **The Tyranny of Mormonism**, Fanny Stenhouse vividly described her friend Mary's terrible ordeal while on the road to Zion. The following has been taken from Mary's letters. "What weary hours we spent!*

Hour after hour went by, mile after mile we walked, and never, never seemed to be a step further on our way ... we traveled slowly, for the carts were always breaking down ... some of the people cut off the tops of their boots and wrapped them around the axles..." Some days they trekked as many as 20 miles, most of the days only a few.

Everyone tried to do their best as they trudged over smothering deserts, waded through muddy streams, and pulled their carts up rugged mountains. When the weather turned cold, the tents leaked and many people became ill or froze to death. One by one the coffins were made as people began to die. Soon they were out of wood and there were no more coffins, just graves.

The children and elderly were the first to drop, and the young adults began to follow. Mary wrote, "As death thinned our ranks, the labours of those who survived increased." By then the people were desperately struggling, the stronger pulling the carts with the weaker ones pushing. As the men began to fall, the women attempted to take their places. Mary wrote, "To be left behind was death ... I saw poor miserable creatures utterly worn out, dying in the arms of other forlorn and hopeless creatures."

The expedition came to a halt in freezing weather a few days out of Salt Lake City. They could no longer travel. A messenger was sent to Brigham Young, who responded with wagons of food and warm clothing. As the people received nourishment and warmth, their spirits improved considerably. A few weeks later, what was left of the group marched courageously into Zion, singing the Push Cart song and praising the Lord. There had been 420 people in the party when it left Iowa City; 353 completed the journey.

For a detailed account of the Handcart Migration, the author recommends the book "**Handcarts to Zion**" by LeRoy and Ann W. Hafen.

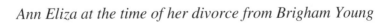

Ann Eliza at the time of her divorce from Brigham Young

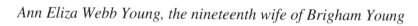

Ann Eliza Webb Young, the nineteenth wife of Brigham Young

Courtesy of The Utah State Historical Society

Brigham Young

Courtesy of The University of Oklahoma

Belle Starr

Chapter 5

BELLE STARR

Petticoat Desperado

O ver a century has passed since Belle Starr, one of America's most daring and glamorous figures, fired the last shot from her pearl-handled revolver, made her last ride, and was murdered by an unknown assailant. Although Belle was raised to be a refined lady, she became a female desperado. It is doubtful that the life of any woman in history can compare to that of the dashing, daring Belle Starr, a woman accepted by men as an equal in the male-dominated society of the late 1800s.

Myra Belle Shirley was born February 5, 1848, in Washington County of northwestern Arkansas. She was the daughter of John and Elizabeth Shirley, members of a wealthy, aristocratic Virginia family. In 1854, when Myra Belle was 6, the Shirleys moved to Carthage, in Jasper County, Missouri, where the family opened a hotel-tavern, livery stables and a blacksmith shop. With the aid of a few slaves, John Shirley also farmed the land, growing his own produce and raising stock.

Myra's father became a leading citizen in Carthage, and was often referred to as the "judge" because of his education and large, impressive library of books. Her mother, Elizabeth, was admired by the local women for her genteel ways, fashion magazines, and a highly polished piano which occupied a large space in her parlor. The Shirleys' hospitality and service were recognized for miles around, and their prominent guests included lawyers, judges and wealthy ranchers.

In these comfortable, refined surroundings Myra Belle led a happy, uncomplicated childhood. She spent most of her time in the company of her two older brothers, Preston, the eldest, and Ed who carried the nickname of "Bud." They taught their little sister how to ride and shoot, and Myra became a familiar sight as she dashed across the fields on her lively mare. On weekdays Myra Belle attended the Carthage Female Academy, where she learned to read and write fluently, eventually becoming an avid reader. She also learned to play her mother's piano and would frequently entertain guests visiting the hotel. The girl was a natural actress and enjoyed being the center of attraction.

This peaceful life, however, came to an end when the Civil War broke out and the Shirleys placed their sympathies with the Southern cause. Belle was only 15 years old when her brother Bud rode away to become a captain with Quantrill's guerrillas. William "Bill" Quantrill was a ruthless man who first fought for the Confederate Army, then used it as an excuse to rob and pillage. When the war ended, his band continued to plunder for personal profit.

It has been said that during the war Myra Belle acted as a scout for Quantrill's band, passing information on to her brother and his comrades. Although she rode sidesaddle, Myra Belle could ride as well as any man, and her sense of adventure made her a valuable addition to Quantrill's guerrillas. Very few suspected the young girl of being a spy, but she did come under suspicion more than once. She was much too smart, however, to get caught carrying messages.

According to legend, Belle was once captured while engaged in a scouting mission. Her captor, Major Eno, advised Belle he was detaining her until his men had time to ride to Carthage and arrest her brother Bud, who was reportedly visiting his parents. The Federal forces held the girl hostage for several hours before releasing her, believing she could not possibly reach her brother in time to warn him. Myra Belle leaped on her horse and set out for Carthage, taking all the short-cuts she knew. She stopped only long enough to cut switches to spur on her horse. The story relates that when the Union troops arrived to pick up Bud Shirley, they were greeted by his younger sister who politely informed them her brother had left a half hour before.

Later that year Bud was killed at Sarcoxie. It was said that Myra Belle and her father went together to claim his body. While John

Shirley tenderly placed the remains of his son in the wagon, Myra Belle grabbed Bud's revolver from its holster and screamed, *"You damned blue-bellies will pay for this."* [1] John sprang to grab his distraught daughter. Before he could reach her, she leveled the revolver at the troops and pulled the trigger—but when the weapon clicked, nothing happened. The caps had been removed.

For the next year the Shirleys lived in an atmosphere of guerrilla warfare. In 1864 Carthage was abandoned by the Union troops that had occupied the town. When the Rebels returned, they ransacked and burned to the ground what remained of Carthage.

The Shirleys turned their backs on the destruction and sold what was left of the once-prosperous property. Still broken-hearted over Bud's death, they loaded their remaining household items into two wagons and headed for Texas to join Preston, John Shirley's oldest son. Myra Belle drove one of the wagons; she was 16 years old. It is believed the family passed within a few miles of what would someday be "Younger's Bend," Belle's hideout for desperadoes.

John Shirley settled on a fertile piece of land near Scyne, Texas, where the family could live as before, farming the land, raising stock and starting a new hotel. Their first home was a simple dugout, later to be replaced with a fine large house. It was located about nine miles east of Dallas, which at the time was a city of dusty streets, saloons and gambling halls.

During the following year Myra Belle blossomed into an attractive young woman of medium build, with dark hair and large expressive brown eyes. Wearing a flaring skirt and man's hat, she presented a vision of youth, not quite beautiful but very fetching. Myra Belle appeared graceful upon her horse and was an expert rider. She still rode sidesaddle as it was considered lady-like, but she was no longer the carefree girl of a few years ago. The war and her brother's death had made many changes.

John Shirley had turned his home into a refuge for the friends of his dead son, so when six horsemen came up the road one evening, it was not unusual. They were all riding excellent mounts with fine Texas saddles. Their leader, a tall, muscular man of about 22, was welcomed at the door by the Shirleys. His name was Cole Younger, the man who was to change the life of Myra Belle.

---

1 **Belle Starr and Her Times**, Glenn Shirley

Myra Belle had never met a man like Cole and she couldn't take her young, inexperienced eyes off of him. Many strangers had visited the Shirleys' home over the past year, but none were as exciting or handsome as the one she had just met. She didn't see the coldness in his blue eyes – only the romance. Myra Belle couldn't have known that this charming stranger read the Bible with a passion and quoted the Twenty-third Psalm as he robbed and pillaged. Cole Younger was the type of man who loved the smell of burned black powder, the thrill of shooting, and the company of fancy ladies.

Cole and Myra Belle were immediately attracted to each other. Belle was ripe for plucking, and Cole was disarmed by her exciting youthfulness. The six men remained at the ranch for several days. When they left, Myra Belle rode out with them, leaving her upset family without a backward glance. She was no longer Myra Belle; she was now Belle, Cole Younger's woman.

They made a handsome couple; but if Cole Younger thought he would make Belle his gang's slave, he was mistaken. She was a high-spirited young woman who rode beside him as an equal, not as his servant. Belle remained with Younger for several months, long enough to learn the thrill of the chase. When she returned home she was pregnant, but not repentant. As expected, Younger denied they had ever been married and said the child was not his. All Belle had to show for the experience was the baby and a pearl-handled revolver that had been given to her by Younger. She kept both.

The Shirleys attempted to hold their heads high and ignore the scorn of their neighbors. In 1867, when Belle was 19, Pearl Younger was born. Belle adored her baby. She would sit and rock little Pearl for hours as she marveled at each tiny feature. The new mother made all kinds of plans for the little bundle in her arms. She even forgot to hate Cole Younger, remembering only their passionate love and the thrill of riding with his band.

Little Pearl eased the pain in the Shirleys' hearts. They too fell in love with the tiny girl. John Shirley stood ready to defend his daughter and granddaughter against the slurs of the community. Shirley had never been accepted by his Texas neighbors. He was an energetic man who was used to living in Missouri where water was plentiful and raising food and livestock were a way of life. When he continued to do this in Texas, where water was scarce, the Texans who grew cotton and grazed cattle called the family "water-hogs." This was added to the vicious gossip about the illegitimate Pearl and her wild mother, Belle.

When Belle was 20, Jim Reed entered her life. He was the son of a farming family the Shirleys had known while living in Missouri. Like Cole Younger, Jim was a close friend of the James boys and had ridden with Quantrill. He was a reticent man who preferred to remain in the background, constantly using aliases. Although Reed appeared to be a peaceful person, he lived by the rule of the Winchester and .45.

There are two versions of the marriage between Belle and Jim Reed. One is that the Shirleys had no objection to their daughter's choice of a husband. They admired Reed because he had been a Confederate soldier who was respected among their neighbors. It was said the couple were married by the Rev. S. Wilkins on November 1, 1866. That would have made Belle 18 at the time of her marriage. It has also been said that Jim Reed, not Cole Younger, fathered Pearl. Yet, Pearl went by the name of Younger.

The other version states that Jim Reed and Belle had a torrid courtship, and John Shirley objected. Fearing his daughter would bring more disgrace upon the family, he locked Belle in her room. Late one night the amorous lover arrived with his gang, placed a ladder beneath Belle's window, and abducted his bride. It was said Jim Reed and Belle were married on horseback, surrounded by 20 bandits as witnesses. The bride was supposed to have carried baby Pearl in her arms and worn a black velvet riding habit. Whatever the true story, Belle and Jim Reed were legally married. As to the identity of Pearl's father, it could have been Cole Younger even though Belle was married to Reed.

Once more, Belle's restless blood had caused her to leave home and become a member of a gang of desperadoes. The newlyweds returned to Missouri, where they temporarily lived with Jim Reed's family. While Belle and baby Pearl captured the hearts of the Reed family, Jim renewed his friendship with Tom Starr, one of the

West's most violent renegades. Starr was a full-blooded Cherokee Indian who stood 6 feet, 7 inches tall and was an expert with the Bowie knife. He lived on Indian territory in Oklahoma with his wife, eight sons, and two daughters. Together they formed the infamous "Starr Clan" and were a source of terror and embarrassment to the Cherokee Nation.

Although Belle became a respected member of the Reed family, there were many suspicions regarding her husband and the way he earned his living. Jim was away most of the time; and in 1869, when Belle was 21, the Reeds were forced to flee Missouri. Jim had become involved in a feud and a warrant for his arrest had been issued. Jim and Belle took Pearl and traveled to California where, some say, Reed worked for a brief time in a gambling house.

Earning an honest living was obviously not Reed's idea of life, for he was soon back at his old profession: robbing stages and stealing horses. Belle had another child, and the couple returned to Texas with their new son named Ed. The Shirleys dearly loved their daughter and granddaughter and accepted Belle's family with open arms. They helped the Reeds to establish themselves on a small ranch. Belle settled down to raise her children, and again Jim started to wander. Soon Belle joined her husband as he rode into the Cherokee lands to buy and sell stolen horses. On one of these frequent trips she met the outlaw Sam Starr, son of the notorious Tom Starr and the man who was destined to become her next husband.

By now Belle enjoyed the life she led and found her children to be an inconvenience. Motherhood meant responsibility, and that meant losing her adventurous spirit. With two children to care for, she could not race over the countryside beside the kind of men she admired. Belle had learned to love the excitement of the chase more than she loved her children. At the age of 25 she left Pearl and Ed with her parents and gained the freedom to again ride with gun-slingers.

Over the years, Belle developed a scathing tongue and rough vocabulary. She kept men under her control with her superior intelligence and pure sex appeal. At a time when most women were meekly bowing to male tyranny, Belle was admired for her freedom and exciting life-style. She became part of the romance of the Early West while the majority of women lived a quiet life. Although there were other women like Belle, none had her flair for the dramatic or the ability to control others. It has been said that Belle would have made a fine actress if she had not become part of Quantrill's band or met Cole Younger. Once she experienced the thrill of living in constant danger, Belle could never return to the refined life she had once led.

Under Belle's guidance, the cattle rustling business became so prosperous that she moved into Dallas, Texas, and opened a livery stable. Her horses were excellent mounts, and no one questioned their source. After all, Belle was married to an ex-Confederate soldier, so the people blamed Reed's problems on the war. Things were going so well that Reed was able to openly visit his wife. The law stepped in once to arrest him, but Belle's objections were so vocal they let him go.

With so much money rolling in, Belle added a stud to her stable and bought a fancy buggy. She dressed in long, black velvet skirts with exquisite lace blouses. She wore a man's Stetson hat adorned with an ostrich plume and carried her six-shooter around her waist in a decorative holster. Mrs. Reed cut a fancy figure dressed in all her finery. At times she would liven up her costumes with a fringed skirt of buckskin, high-topped boots, and a necklace of rattlesnake rattles. Belle drank whiskey at the bar and played poker with the boys. She didn't smoke because it was not considered refined.

It was said that Belle had an evil eye and, although she never had a shoot-out with a man, she was female enough to have a man do the killing for her. While Reed was away Belle enjoyed the company of many lovers, including Cole Younger who would travel to Texas every so often to visit the notorious lady. All of Belle's men were large and dark. She seemed to prefer Indians.

Belle brought Pearl to live with her for a brief period. Although she had left her daughter with the Shirleys, Belle still adored the child and called her "Rosie." Like all proud mothers, Belle believed her daughter was destined to be famous and she decided to make her an actress. She hired the best teachers in Dallas to train Pearl and even managed to get her on the vaudeville stage.

Unfortunately, the little girl collapsed from a brain hemorrhage the night of her first performance, which ended what could have been a theatrical career. Following that unpleasant experience, Pearl was returned to the home of her grandparents.

While returning home from a robbery in the summer of 1875, Reed was shot to death by a man named John Morris. The gunman had pretended to be Reed's friend, but all he wanted was the reward for Reed's capture. Since Reed was a stranger in that town, someone had to identify the body before the reward could be collected. A message was sent to Belle to inform her of her husband's death. When she received word to collect his remains, Belle knew Morris had killed Reed for the reward. She was determined to prevent Morris from receiving the money. As Belle entered the room where the body lay, she calmly looked at the corpse and without the least sign of emotion told the men that someone had killed the wrong man. Then as she turned and left the room she looked at Morris and told him he would have to kill Jim Reed if he wanted the reward for his body. Her husband was buried in a potter's field; and if Belle felt any remorse, she hid it well.

In 1876 the law finally caught up with Cole Younger. He was sentenced to life in the Minnesota State Penitentiary. Belle had never lost the affection she felt for her first love, and for the first time in her life she felt alone. That, however, was temporary. She immediately set up housekeeping with a man called Blue Duck, a young Indian she could easily manipulate. She also gathered around her a group of male admirers as reckless as herself. They were men like Jack Spaniard and Jim French, both outlaws who also became her lovers.

For the next few years Belle and her desperadoes rustled cattle and robbed banks and stagecoaches. She could outride, outshoot, and outsmart most men. Belle had the ability to arrange the release of prisoners through parole or pardon. She knew how to avoid the federal marshals and the Indian Patrol, and she could easily dispose of stolen property and illegal whiskey. Belle became known as the "Bandit Queen," and she was the brains behind the gang, usually remaining in the background. Although Belle was arrested many times, she managed to keep her freedom, leaving behind her a string of robberies and lovers; both of which she shrugged off.

Once, when Belle was arrested for a minor crime, a wealthy stockman saw her and was physically attracted. When he asked how much it would cost to get her case dismissed, she said $2,500. He sold some cattle and gave her the cash. A few days later Belle was released for a nominal fine, leaving her with a profit of $2,490. The amorous rancher spent the evening with the charming lady and then asked her to return the rest of the money. When she said no, his friends advised the man — who was uncommonly ugly and overly romantic — to sue her for fraud. His noble reply was, *"Hell! Let her keep it. I reckon with what she's had to put up with, she's earned every cent of it."* [1]

In 1878 Belle once again found herself under arrest for horse stealing. Not only was the deputy jailer charmed into releasing her, he eloped with her. After a month the exhausted deputy returned to Dallas, confessing he had worked like a slave — cooking, fetching, and romancing — for the woman. Later, to his embarrassment, he found a note pinned to his coat. It read, *"Released because found unsatisfactory."* [2]

In 1880 Belle decided to find a permanent mate, one who was attractive and sexually durable. She chose Sam Starr, the young outlaw son of the notorious Tom Starr. Sam was three-quarters Cherokee, tall and muscular, with long, black hair cut off below his neck and tied with a scarlet ribbon. Sam dressed like a white man, possessed a magnetic personality, and was good-looking. Although he was four years younger than Belle, he appeared older. It seemed to be a fine match.

When Sam brought Belle to meet his father, Tom Starr, who had been advised to kill Belle as he would a snake, the elder Starr also fell under her spell. Perhaps underneath it all both Tom and Belle were alike: ruthless and cunning. Sam and Belle were married in the eyes of the Cherokee Nation and settled on Sam's 1,000 acres of tribal land. Belle called it "Younger's Bend."

The couple built a two-room log cabin on a strategic site at the edge of the Canadian River. A series of hills could be seen across the river, and to the north there was a large mountain range. The only entrance to the cabin was over a winding, wooded trail through

1 **Western History Collection**, University of Oklahoma

2 1938, **Western History Collection**, University of Oklahoma

a canyon and across a meadow. Anyone approaching could be easily seen, and the hills and rugged mountains created a perfect place to hide the desperadoes who sought refuge. Belle added two cabins, one for guests and the other for outlaws. She decorated the home with a few feminine touches and fancy furniture. Sam Starr was quite pleased and agreed to anything that made his squaw happy.

Belle brought Pearl home to live with her, and the Starrs began raising cattle and farming their land. It was a content family. Belle bought herself a fine black mare she named "Venus," an ornate saddle, and a brace of ivory-handled Colt .45 revolvers. She even had a piano hauled in over the treacherous trail, and the sound of music could be heard ringing out over the hills.

Pearl, who was about 13, loved Younger's Bend, and her mother soon named her the "Canadian Lily." Mother and daughter devised a special game they enjoyed playing together. They would listen to the chirping of the various birds and each would claim a bird as her own. A blue-jay would be Belle's; a Bob White, Pearl's. The game lasted through the day. In the fall they would gather pine cones to decorate the mantel at the cabin. They were both excellent horsewomen and would ride over the hills together, occasionally visiting another family. The Starrs were civil to their neighbors because they didn't want any trouble. Younger's Bend had become a hiding place for notorious bandits; even Jesse James visited a couple of times.

In 1883 Belle and Sam Starr were arrested for stealing horses. The news was telegraphed all over the nation. Belle was called "The Petticoat Terror of the Plains," a name that remained with her the rest of her life. The couple was tried before Judge Isaac C. Parker. Belle had appeared before him already and would do so again. Judge Parker was the federal judge of the U.S. District Court at Fort Smith, Arkansas. He made no allowances; his sentences were firm. During his time on the bench, Parker tried 13,000 cases and found 9,000 guilty. He sentenced 172 men and hanged 88. [1] He was called the "hanging judge" and was known to be cruel. When they finally abolished his court he had nothing more to live for and died the same year.

---

1 **Belle Starr, The Bandit Queen**, Burton Rascoe

Following the trial a local newspaper carried this story: *"... The very idea of a woman being charged with an offense of this kind and that she was the leader of a band of horse thieves and wielding a power over them as their queen and guiding spirit was sufficient to fill the courtroom with spectators during the trial, which lasted four days, the jury finding a verdict of guilty against them ..."* [1]

The Starrs were sentenced to nine months in jail at Fort Smith. The only time Belle showed any emotion during the prosecution was when she said she had once been married to Jim Reed. She wrote a long letter to Pearl, who had been sent to live with friends, promising to bring the girl and her brother Ed home when she and Sam were released. She also said they would live together as a happy family.

While in prison Belle wove chair bottoms out of cane and became friends with the warden and his wife. She knew how to be sociable and could win anyone over when it pleased her. Because of this friendship, Belle's stay in jail was pleasant, and she received an early release. Sam had to serve his full sentence, spending his time at hard labor.

True to her word, when Belle was released she brought both her children to live at Younger's Bend; and when Sam returned they managed to stay out of trouble for a while. The couple even appeared at the county fair, where they gave several performances portraying a battle between outlaws and Indians. It seemed that time in jail had rehabilitated the Starrs.

This good behavior was not to last, however. Sam and Belle once again began to roam the territory in search of horses and whatever else they could steal. The desperadoes continued to ride in to Younger's Bend and Belle relieved her boredom by planning new, more daring raids. She also met John Middleton, a 25-year-old visitor who had been riding with Billy the Kid. Middleton, a fancy dresser with a fine muscular build, soon became a member of the gang of outlaws. He was wanted for many crimes, including murder, and had a $1,500 price on his head. Sam had to leave Younger's Bend soon after Middleton joined the Starrs, and Middleton became Belle's lover in Sam's absence.

This love affair did not last long. A few days after Sam returned,

---

1 Fort Smith New Era, Feb. 23, 1883, **Western History Collection**, University of Oklahoma

Middleton's body with half of his face missing was found floating in the river. It was assumed he had drowned, and the authorities recorded it as an accidental death. It was said that Sam found out about Belle's indiscretion and shot Middleton in cold blood. Others claimed Belle had tired of the man and murdered him herself.

Meanwhile, Pearl had taken a lover and found she was expecting a child. Belle was furious; she couldn't understand how her sweet baby could do this to her! Things were not going well at Younger's Bend. Even Belle's son Ed was becoming defiant. Many times Belle had to whip him with her riding quirt to keep the boy in line. Later that year, 1886, when Belle was 38, the Starrs attended a party at a neighbor's home and Sam Starr was killed. He and another man had tried to settle an old score, and each shot the other to death. At the time of his death Sam was wanted by the U.S. Marshal for robbing a post office and rustling cattle. The Choctaw and Cherokee Indians were also looking for him for robbing the Creek Nation's treasury. Although Belle had probably planned the crimes, she was not arrested.

Following Sam's death, Belle "married" Jim July, a well-educated, tall and handsome, 24-year-old Indian. They lived together at Younger's Bend, which meant they were legally married under Cherokee law. This marriage provided Belle with a permanent lover and enabled her to keep her property, which would have reverted to the Cherokee Nation. Jim July was one of Sam's cousins, and at Belle's request he assumed the name of Jim July Starr. Belle was 16 years older than July. He was four years older than Pearl and seven years older than Belle's son Ed. It was a complicated situation.

It became even more complicated when Pearl gave birth to a baby girl. Belle didn't want anything to do with the child who was named Flossie, so Pearl left her daughter with relatives. Everything was going wrong for Belle. The same year Flossie was born, Belle was accused of harboring criminals; but the complaint was dismissed. Later that year Ed was arrested for larceny and sentenced to seven years at the Federal Penitentiary. Belle could have arranged for his release, but she felt he needed to learn a lesson. Although she eventually had her son paroled, Ed Reed never forgave his mother for letting him go to jail. When he was released he returned to Younger's Bend, surly and jealous of July.

Ed was never an easy person to handle, and Belle was very hard on the young man. One of the worst beatings she gave him happened during a tantrum of rage when she discovered Ed had ridden her favorite horse against her orders. Belle picked up her riding quirt, woke the boy from a sound sleep, and slashed his back to raw flesh. Following this merciless beating, Ed disappeared. It has been said that Belle had an incestuous relationship with her son, which would explain his jealousy of Jim July.

No doubt all of this and Jim July weighed heavily on Belle's mind the fateful evening of February 3, 1889 — two days before her 41st birthday — as she returned home alone from Fort Smith. July had been charged with larceny. Belle had talked him into surrendering to the law, pointing out that since the case against him was weak, the judge would have to set him free. Knowing her husband was upset, Belle had ridden halfway to the fort with him, then had turned her mare around to head for Younger's Bend. As she circled the field of a neighbor, Edgar Watson, a shotgun roared out from the fence corner, sending a charge of buckshot into Belle's back. She fell from her horse, sliding into a muddy pool of water on the trail. Then the murderer walked up and shot her twice more with Belle's own revolver.

Pearl was sent to bring her mother's body home to Younger's Bend. The neighbor women washed Belle's body, anointed it with oil and peppermint, and dressed her in a black silk dress with a fancy white collar. Belle's hands were crossed, holding her favorite six-shooter, the same one Cole Younger had given her so many years before.

They placed Belle's remains in a plain board coffin. The ceremony was a quiet one. Those who attended were Jim July who was released from Fort Smith for the funeral, Pearl and Ed, a few friends, white squatters, outlaws, Choctaws and Cherokees, and many people who were just curious. No prayers were read. As the mourners passed in review, each Cherokee placed a small piece of cornbread in the coffin, following an ancient tribal custom.

The question of who murdered Belle Starr has never been

solved. Following the funeral, her neighbor Watson was charged with the murder and remained in jail for several weeks. This no doubt saved him from the outlaws who were in town to avenge Belle's death. Many people spoke kindly of Belle and said she had visited their homes, had cooked meals when the women were ill, and had always been kind to their children.

Although there was bad blood between Watson and Belle, he was found innocent. Belle had a way of extracting information out of people then holding it over their heads to make them do as she requested. She knew Watson was wanted for murder in another state and she also had an argument with him over some land. That made Watson a prime suspect.

Jim July Starr also could have murdered her for convincing him to give himself up to face charges in Fort Smith. It was said he could have doubled back over the trail and shot his own wife, then went on to Fort Smith. It was also rumored that he had found a younger woman and knew Belle would never have let him free.

Jim Middleton, brother of her former lover John Middleton, has also been added to the list of suspects because he could have murdered Belle to avenge his brother's death. Then there was her own son Ed, who hated her for her cruelty. People continue to come forward with new evidence, and the question still remains: who murdered Belle Starr? Meanwhile, the notorious woman lies quietly in her grave at Younger's Bend.

Pearl had an ornate tombstone erected for her mother. It had a carved picture of Belle's favorite mare Venus at the top, and a small star and clasped hand holding a flower at the bottom. The inscription reads:

———————◆———————

Shed not for her the bitter tear,
Nor give the heart to vain regret;
Tis but the casket that lies here,
The gem that filled it sparkles yet.

◆———————————————◆

THE LEGACY OF BELLE STARR

Although Belle would not be considered attractive by today's standards, she has been portrayed as an exciting female who was sought after for her beauty and sex appeal. Numerous books have been written about the legendary Belle Starr, and in 1883 Richard Fox's **Police Gazette** *immortalized her as a female Robin Hood and Jesse James. In 1941 Twentieth-Century Fox produced the movie* **Belle Starr, the Bandit Queen** *starring Gene Tierney as Belle and Dana Andrews as Sam Starr, further enhancing the legend of this extremely complex woman.*

Belle's daughter Pearl let a respectable family adopt Flossie, had a brief marriage, and eventually drifted into prostitution. Later she became a madame and opened her own "house," which she operated for 23 years. She was known as Pearl Starr.

Belle's son Ed Reed became a deputy marshal, married a Cherokee school teacher, and for a few years was a fine officer of the law. One night in 1896 he drank too much whiskey and was shot to death in a quarrel with a saloon owner.

Jim July Starr was shot in 1890 by Deputy Marshal Bob Hutchens, who believed July had murdered Belle Starr. The deputy was only 18 years old and wanted to avenge Belle's death because he admired the woman.

Cole Younger was released from prison in 1901 and became a tombstone salesman. He eventually received a full pardon and organized the "Cole Younger-Frank James Wild West Show." Younger died in 1916. He was 72 at the time of his death.

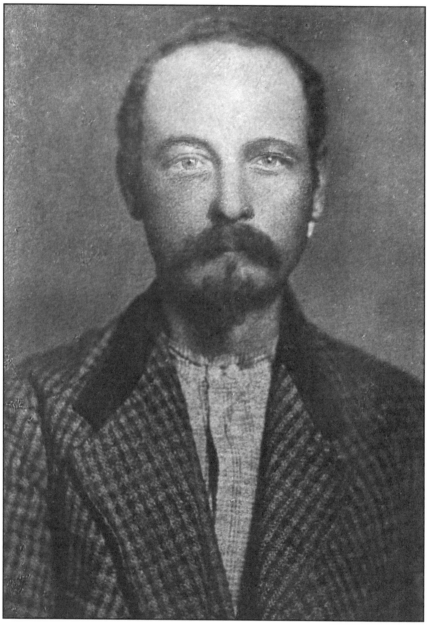

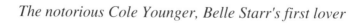

The notorious Cole Younger, Belle Starr's first lover

Belle Starr

*America's most noted female bandit and the first white
woman to live in the Oklahoma Territory*

*An older Belle Starr with one of her young lovers,
the Blue Duck*

NEWSPAPER ARTICLE BY BELLE STARR

"The following sketch of her life was written by Belle Starr and handed to a reporter of this paper over two years ago, but we never had occasion to use it. We publish it now verbatim (sic), as an evidence of her intelligence and education!"

The Indian Arrow, *Feb. 21, 1889*
Fort Gibson, Texas, p. 4, col. 1-4
Courtesy of The Oklahoma Historical Society

"After a more adventurous life than generally falls into the lot of women, I settled permanently in the Indian Territory, selecting a place of picturesque beauty on the Canadian River. There, far from society, I hoped to pass the remainder of my life in peace and quietude. So long had I been estranged from the society of women (whom I thoroughly detest) that I thought I would find it irksome to live in their midst. So I selected a place that but few have ever had the gratification of gossiping around. For a short time I lived very happily in the society of my little girl and husband, a Cherokee Indian, a son of the noted Tom Starr. But it soon became noised around that I was a woman of some notoriety from Texas, from that time on my home and actions have been severely criticized. My home became famous as an outlaw's ranche (sic) long before I was visited by any of the boys who were friends of mine. Indeed, I have never corresponded with any of my old associates and was desirous my whereabouts should be unknown to them. Through rumor they learned of it. Jessie (sic) James first came in, and remained several weeks. He was unknown to my husband, and he never knew until

long afterwards that our home had been honored by Jessie's presence. I introduced Jessie as one Mr. Williams, from Texas. But few outlaws have visited my home, notwithstanding so much has been said. The best people in the country are friends of mine. I have considerable ignorance to cope with, consequently my troubles originate mostly in that quarter. Surrounded by a low down class of shoddy whites who have made the Indian Territory their home to evade paying taxes on their logs and who I will not permit to hunt on my premises, I am the constant theme of their slanderous tongues. In all the world there is no woman more persecuted than I." — Belle Starr

Belle Starr's grave and cabin at Younger's Bend.

Miss Nellie Cashman

Chapter 6

NELLIE CASHMAN

The Irish Angel of Mercy

Nellie Cashman was the type of woman who became part of the legend of the early West. She was a non-conformist, always ready for adventure and willing to lend a hand to the needy. Although Nellie was only 5 feet tall and weighed less than 100 pounds, she was loved from Tombstone to Alaska for her compassion and bravery. Unfortunately, no biography has been written about this inspirational woman and her deeds. The following chapter has been taken from numerous newspaper articles dating back to the turn of the century, supplemented by short stories describing various periods in her life.

Nellie was born in the small seaport of Queenstown, Ireland, in 1851. She immigrated with her older sister Frances to the United States soon after the Civil War. The sisters arrived in Boston, Massachusetts, in 1867 when Nellie was 16 years old. A year later they took a transcontinental train to San Francisco, California, where in 1870 Frances married Thomas Cunningham.

There is no valid record of Nellie Cashman until 1874 when, it is believed, poverty and hard times prompted her to sign on as cook for a party of prospectors on their way to the Cassiar District in the mountains of Juneau, Alaska. At that time Nellie was an attractive, unattached woman of 23 with an Irish flair that let men know she was a no-nonsense woman.

Nellie and the miners traveled to an area new and unexplored, and reportedly rich in ore. They journeyed over rough terrain, many miles from civilization, before setting up camp. Nellie did the cooking and soon began to help with the mining. Working beside the men in "The Land of the Midnight Sun," Nellie Cashman discovered the thrill of prospecting.

In the fall of that year, Nellie left the camp for Victoria, British Columbia, and upon her arrival learned that a fierce winter storm had trapped the men she left behind. They had exhausted their supply of vegetables, and many were seriously ill with scurvy. The resourceful Nellie hired six men, purchased potatoes and vegetables, and headed back to her friends. In one of her newspaper interviews she said that although the weather was severe, her group pushed on over the long difficult trail, reaching the camp in time to save the lives of the prospectors. That trip won the hearts of the Cassiar miners, who remained her friends for life, and Nellie became known as "The Angel of Cassiar."

Nellie never lingered in one place for any amount of time. In 1878 she turned up in the mining camps of Virginia City and Pioche, Nevada. Sometimes she prospected for gold. Other times she cooked; but wherever she went, Nellie always worked. Despite her travels around the mining camps, where most women had a dubious reputation, the purity of Nellie's womanhood was never questioned. Her character and conduct commanded respect.

In 1879, Nellie Cashman decided to move to Arizona, as mining in Nevada was declining. She initially arrived in Tucson, which in those days resembled a Mexican pueblo, with few white women numbered among its citizenry. The founding editor of the *Tombstone Epitaph*, John P. Clum, described his first impression of Nellie in his booklet, *Nellie Cashman*. He was working the day she appeared to place an advertisement for her latest enterprise, the Delmonico Restaurant, and he wrote, *"One morning a lady visited my office and arranged for the ad posted above. It was in this matter-of-fact business fashion that I first met Nellie Cashman ... Nellie was the first of her sex to embark solo in a business enterprise. Her frank manner, her self-reliant spirit, and her emphatic and fascinating Irish brogue impressed me very much, and indicated that she was a woman of strong character and marked individuality ..."* She left a lasting impression upon Clum; and since he was a wanderer himself, they became good friends.

The following year, when news of the silver strike in Tombstone reached Nellie's ears, she hired a few hands and moved her restaurant to the town that was considered "too tough to die." There in Tombstone, Nellie set down what few roots she possessed and bought a large building called the Russ House, converting it into a restaurant and hotel. Nellie's place soon became as famous as the Bird Cage Saloon and the O.K. Corral. She fed and housed newcomers free-of-charge if they couldn't afford to pay and was constantly grubstaking impoverished miners. Nellie always declared, *"There are no cockroaches in my kitchen, and the flour is clean,"* and charged double for her meals. That, however, did not cause her to lose any customers. The men knew that this diminutive young woman, with her dark hair and sparkling eyes, would give most of the money she earned back to the community in some way.

"Among her clientele in Tombstone were Doc Holliday, Johnny Ringo, Pat Garrett and Wyatt Earp. Nellie never carried a pistol or gun, claiming the 'boys' would see to it that anyone who insulted her would never live to repeat the offense." [1]

There were many needs in Tombstone, and Nellie attempted to attend to them all. She was generous and self-sacrificing, willing to help with an illness or give to a worthy cause. In his book, Clum wrote, *"If she asked for a contribution — we contributed. If she had tickets to sell — we bought tickets. If she needed actors for a play — we volunteered to act. And, although Nellie's pleas were frequent, none ever refused her. In fact, we would have felt offended had we not been allowed an opportunity to assist in some way in each one of Nellie's benefits."* To Nellie, who was a devout Catholic, giving was more than religious zeal; she felt it was her sacred duty.

In 1880 Nellie's sister Frances was widowed and left penniless with five children to support. Nellie immediately rushed to San Francisco and returned to Tombstone with the bereaved family. Three years later Frances died and "Aunt Nell" took the five orphans, ranging from 4 to 12 years of age, under her generous wing. She played baseball, baked pies, and nursed the children through their illnesses. No matter what she did or where she went, Nellie would take her family along or leave her young charges with responsible people. Before the children grew up, they had lived in mountain cabins as far away as Montana and Wyoming. They knew Aunt Nell was often a prospector and respected her for her hard work. She provided a fine role model for the growing youngsters.

Daily Colonist, Victoria, B.C., 1898

Although Nellie was a staunch Catholic, she would go out in the dark of night to minister to anyone in need regardless of sect or creed. In 1882 she contributed funds from her own purse to build Tombstone's Catholic church. Many nights she was also seen gently helping Father Gallegher safely home after the old priest had consumed a "wee drop too many." Nellie treated the red-light ladies and the prisoners in jail with the same kindness she showed the so-called respectable people. Everyone was alike to her.

Nellie demonstrated her love for the unfortunate when five convicted murderers were to be simultaneously executed on the same scaffold. It was rumored that a grandstand was being built so the curious could pay to see the hangings. Although the murders were committed in cold blood and the men deserved to be hanged, Nellie thought it was an outrage upon human decency for anyone to profit from the executions. She enlisted several men on behalf of the prisoners, and in the early morning hours they demolished the grandstand, with Nellie striking the first blow. *"People should die with dignity,"* she exclaimed, and she was sincerely interested in the souls of the men. Nellie was so concerned that before the hangings she assumed the role of mother confessor to the two convicted Catholic prisoners and converted the other three. She also saw that the men's bodies were not sent to a medical school for dissection by students. Each night for several weeks after the burial, two miners could be seen carrying a coffee pot as they took their silent vigil beside the graves.

Several months later another emergency occurred when Nellie saved the life of E.B. Gage, superintendent of the Grand Central Mining Company. The price of silver had decreased and the mine reduced wages by 50 cents a day, resulting in a bitter strike among the workers. The situation became so serious that the embittered miners planned to kidnap and lynch the superintendent. Nellie got out her buggy and went to visit the Gage home. After a brief visit, she drove leisurely through Tombstone, then whipped her horses on to the railroad station, where the intended victim left his hiding place in the back of the buggy and safely boarded a train.

In 1884 a Mexican prospector stopped by the Russ House to show Nellie a gold nugget he found in Baja California, and she then decided to go to Mexico. Dressed in overalls and boots, Nellie, and a group of hastily assembled men, departed. The eager prospectors hired a boat to take them to Muleje, Mexico, and upon arrival went in search of gold. They had not realized the weather would be so hot, and in their haste they neglected to carry enough water. Once again Nellie came to the rescue. She was in better physical shape than the men, so she left them, promising to return with water. A few days later, Miss Cashman arrived with Mexican helpers carrying goatskin containers of water on the backs of burros. Subsequently, the miners and Nellie did not find gold, so they abandoned the trip.

On their return voyage, the captain of the boat became half-crazed from an overabundance of alcohol. Since the passengers' lives were in danger, the miners, with Nellie's help, bound the man with a rope and stowed him below the decks for safekeeping. When the boat docked at Guaymus, officials arrested Nellie and her men for capturing the captain, and threw them in the local prison. The miners and their fearless female companion languished in the foul-smelling, unsanitary jail until the American consul obtained a release.

Whether it was adventure, the search for gold, or a good deed, the modest appearing Nellie Cashman was always ready to participate. Everywhere she went, her Celtic accent and tempestuous spirit were admired. Although small in stature, her Irish temper proved large. One man claimed she was *"the wildest young woman I ever met,"* and as she grew older, her contemporaries often referred to Nellie Cashman as an "Old Sour Dough" or "The Old Time Prospector."

Nellie never married, and if she had any love life she kept it to herself. She preferred the company of men over women; and once when interviewed about marriage, Nellie said, with a twinkle in her eye, *"Why I haven't had the time for marriage. Men are a nuisance anyway."* She then explained that she preferred being pals with men to being a cook for one man, and she found them always ready to play square with women who worked among them. *"But you can't take advantage of them,"* she continued, *"Some women in business think they should be given special favors because of their sex. Well all I can say after years of experience is that those special favors spell doom to a woman in her business. It just gives me a great deal of pride to go back to every place I've ever been and look folks square in the eye and know I've paid my bills and played the game like a man."* [1]

Nellie Cashman could never be classed as an old maid; she was more of a bachelor maid, who loved to travel and was constantly looking for excitement and challenge.

In 1898, when Nellie was 47, mining in Tombstone began to fade, and her children had all grown to maturity. There was no reason to remain in Arizona, so Nellie returned to Alaska and settled in Dawson, where she opened the Can-Can restaurant. She also started a small store in her basement. At that time Dawson was a wild and wooly mining camp at the peak of its boom and filled with adventurers. When Nellie discovered there was no place for the miners to visit except the bars, she cheerfully turned her basement store into The Prospectors' Haven of Rest. The room was equipped for reading and writing, with free cigars and coffee.

"It was once remarked that whenever Nellie Cashman entered a room in Dawson, those sitting rose to their feet. For if the miners showered the dance hall girls with nuggets and cash, they reserved their most honest gift — respect — for 'Nellie Pioche'..." [2]

While in Dawson, Nellie and her old friend John Clum met once again. Clum was passing through on business and was busily involved in changing the film from his camera in a darkroom when he heard her distinct Irish brogue. Nellie was requesting the photographer to buy a subscription to aid the local Sisters' Hospital; she hadn't changed a bit! Clum wrote, *"Nellie was robust, active, prosperous and popular — even as she was wont to be in those early days of Tombstone."* He also described an amusing incident which occurred in front of her establishment in Dawson during a British holiday: a loyal British miner approached the busy lady and initiated the encounter. *"I say, Nellie, where's your flag?"* he asked. *"Outside,"* she meekly replied. *"Beg pardon, but it's not. I didn't see a Union Jack when I came in,"* the man said. Nellie took his arm and led him to the porch. She pointed to the Stars and Stripes hanging from the wall, above which, in neat arrangement, were

1 **Arizona Star**, January 11, 1925
2 **Daily Colonist**, Victoria, B.C., 1898

small British postage stamps bearing the Union Jack. *"There's my flag,"* she said, then pointed to the stamps upon the wall and said, *"And there's yours!"* The British miner and the Irish lady with a twinkle in her eye joined together in a big laugh.

From that time on, Nellie spent most of her life in Alaska, mining and operating restaurants. Occasionally she returned to the states to visit her adopted children. Although she was broke many times, Nellie never had a problem finding friends to supply her with enough money to get into business. They knew she would give most of it to charity and considered their loans indirect donations.

Nellie hated crowds of people and as a result is credited with being the first woman prospector in the Alaska Territory. She liked the cold, and the hardships acted as a stimulus to her high-spirited nature. While in her 60s Nellie would travel 12 miles by snowshoe to lay in supplies and pick up her mail. Her cabin in Alaska was located 500 miles from cities and towns. One of her special pleasures was drinking black coffee while fixing biscuits and salt pork for breakfast. The company of other women, with their social clubs, and the noise of banging trolley cars, were not for her. It was the sound of the howling dog at midnight and the beauty of nature she loved.

When she was 70 years old, in 1921, Nellie was still mushing (running behind a dog sled), and she set a record that year as champion musher of the world. She mushed her dog team and sled 750 miles in 17 days, breaking her own trail the entire distance from Koyukuk to Seward, Alaska.

On one of Nellie's last visits to the states, her nephew, Mike Cunningham, fondly remembered when Aunt Nell visited him in Bisbee, Arizona, in the early 1920s. Nellie, who was carrying a small bag (she always traveled lightly), stepped down from the train and asked how much the taxi fare was to Cunningham's home. When the driver replied 75 cents, she laughed and said she would rather walk. The driver was so startled that he hurried after her and drove Nellie to her destination free of charge. Later, when her nephew bought a "new-fangled" automobile, Aunt Nell refused to ride in his "dangburn autymobile," claiming she preferred a team of dogs and a sled. They were quieter and easier to handle.

During the visit, Mike encouraged Aunt Nell to remain with him and his family in Arizona, where they could look after her. But his efforts were in vain. Nellie insisted that she return to her staunch friends in Alaska who needed her help. So once again this intrepid woman headed north to search for gold and excitement in the faraway territory of Alaska. Although she had refused Mike's request to stay with him, he saw to it that she was well provided for. Nellie, however, was self-reliant to the end and did not touch a penny until she could no longer care for herself.

In 1924 Nellie became ill in her cabin at Coldfoot and was taken down the river to Fairbanks. At the hospital, it was discovered that Nellie had double pneumonia. The doctors were amazed that she had even survived the trip; but Nellie not only survived, she recovered. She left the hospital in good spirits, determined to find that gold she had spent her life seeking. However, the hardships and toll of the years had sapped her strength. Nellie was soon back in the hospital, that she had helped build, in Victoria, British Columbia. She realized her health had deserted her, and knew the end was near. On January 4, 1925, at the age of 74, Nellie Cashman calmly passed away at St. Joseph's hospital. She was buried next to the Catholic Nuns Plot at Ross Bay Cemetery in Victoria.

The Daily Colonist, in Victoria, B.C., published the following in a September 2, 1962 column. *"Nellie took over $100,000 from one claim, spending every penny buying other claims, looking for more riches. She gave away fortunes, because if any miner was broke and hungry, she would share her wealth."*

The story of Nellie Cashman has been made possible through newspaper stories from the Arizona Historical Society, the University of Arizona, the British Columbia Archives and Records, and the booklet "Nellie Cashman" by John P. Clum, courtesy of the Arizona Historical Society.

Note: The portrait of Nellie Cashman is featured on the cover of this book.

MISS NELLIE CASHMAN

Miss Nellie Cashman: — "Frequent illusion has been made in this column to the indomitable female, who started upon the ice of the Stickeen River in company with two men for Dease Creek. She is a native of Limerick, Ireland, aged about 22, rather pretty and possesses all the vivacity as well as the push and energy inherent to her race. She was one of the few white women who reached Cassiar last year, where she opened a boarding house on Dease Creek and realized a comfortable 'pile.' Her extraordinary freak of attempting to reach the diggings in midwinter and in the face of dangers and obstacles which shipwrecked even the stout-hearted Fannen and thrice drove him back to Wrangel for shelter is attributed by her friends as insanity. So impressed with this idea was the Commander at Fort Wrangel that he sent out a guard of soldiers to bring her back. The guard found her encamped on the ice of Stickeen cooking her evening meal by the heat of a wood fire and humming a lively air. So happy, contented and comfortable did she appear that the 'boys' in blue sat down and took tea at her invitation, and returned without her. It is feared that she has perished from the intense cold that prevailed during the latter part of January along the entire coast."

Daily British Colonist, Victoria, B.C.,
February 5, 1875, p. 3, col. 1.

Nolan Creek, Alaska   *April 15th, 1923*

My dear Mike

I arrived here on the 7th of April. I came over the mountains on a fast dog train and a native driver. The Northern Commercial Co. had every thing arranged for me. The sled only turn over once. I had a little roll in the snow. I didn't see the party that I wanted in New York he was in Florida. I will see you late in the fall. I will remain here five months. I left my clothes at Fairbanks. I came over the mountains very light. I hope the girls will arrive home safely. I had 3 letters from Ellen. She tells me they can speak French very good. Every town in Alaska is looking very good. I hope Willie is getting better. I will see him next winter. I do hope that yourself and the children are in good health. I am feeling fine after my long trip. It is snowing here today. We don't expect the breakup not before the middle of May (That is the spring breakup of ice on the creek). I am fixing up my cabin. I didn't move up from Wiseman. I will go up in a weeks time then the cabin will be fixed and wood cut. My dear I've taken good care of myself. I got off the river before the breakup came and believe me I got off of it in a hurry. Mike drop me a line and let me know how yourself and the children are. I remain my dear Mike your Loving Auntie

Nellie Cashman

Note from Glenn Boyer: Wiseman is on the Koyokuk River straight North of Fairbanks almost and about 190 miles as the crow flies.

A letter from Nellie Cashman to her nephew Mike, courtesy of the Arizona Historical Society.

*In Nellie's later years, she was referred to as an
"Old Sour Dough."*

Courtesy of the Nevada Historical Society

Historian Jeanne Elizabeth Wier

Chapter 7

JEANNE ELIZABETH WIER
◆————————————————————————◆

Northern Nevada's Noted Historian

T he importance of preserving history was the driving force behind this indefatigable woman of the turn of the century. Jeanne Elizabeth Wier knew that a collection of historical material should be gathered and placed within a museum to be enjoyed by future generations. She dedicated most of her life to this cause. This remarkable woman traveled over rough roads and visited isolated communities as she searched throughout Nevada, digging for old documents and extracting promises from pioneers that they would collect their memoirs for posterity.

Jeanne Elizabeth Wier was born April 8, 1870, in Grinnell, Iowa. She was a well-educated woman who had studied at Stanford University, where she received her degree. Jeanne taught school in Iowa, her home state, and served as an assistant principal in an Oregon high school. She came to the Nevada State College (now the University of Nevada) in 1899 as a temporary replacement in the college history department. While at the college, Jeanne developed an avid interest in the preservation of her adopted state's history. She later became a suffragist and feminist and took a leave of absence for advanced studies at Columbia University.

After completing her studies, Jeanne returned to Nevada, and became actively involved in the formation of the Nevada State Historical Society. In 1904 she was elected secretary and curator. It was the society's only "professional" office, at which she remained until her death in 1950. As a historian, Jeanne was aware that the pioneers of Nevada were rapidly passing away. She set out upon the difficult task of collecting and cataloging everything she could gather.

The following story, supplemented by selected quotes, has

been taken from the 1908 diary of Jeanne Elizabeth Wier. It provides a graphic insight to the days of the early West. Jeanne tells of her interesting experiences while traveling by train, buckboard, and foot as she made her way across the state, securing material for future Nevadans.

Jeanne's trip started Wednesday, July 15, 1908, when she left Reno for Goldfield, Nevada, traveling by train in a hot upper berth. Upon reaching her destination, Jeanne was forced to wait until Friday for a train to Las Vegas. While in Goldfield she gathered old photographs and certificates. On July 17 she left at 10:10 a.m. for Las Vegas and attempted to eat lunch at Rhyolite but found the weather too hot for food. When she arrived at Las Vegas, Jeanne was taken to the Hotel Charleston, where she had to barricade her door because there were no locks. The kitchen and dining room were one, and the temperature was 100 degrees. She dined on strawberries and tea. The next day Jeanne went to the Stewart Ranch for a visit with Mrs. Stewart and took a team to what was once Ragtown, a community of 1,500 people.

Jeanne returned to the ranch July 20, and spent three days viewing historical sites and going over relics with Mrs. Stewart. Miss Wier left Las Vegas for Panaca, where she was forced to carry two heavy valises all day because the porter failed to check her baggage. The weather was very hot and humid. When Jeanne arrived she found the lodging house closed, so she stayed with a family of which she wrote, *"Given guest parlor. No screens on windows. Flies a million thick and room so musty cannot keep windows closed."*

On Sunday, July 26, Jeanne rose at 3:30 a.m. and left at 4:00 for Pioche, where she wrote, *"Went to Cecil, a dilapidated old hotel ... Flies so bad that went to store and got tanglefoot. Hotel in keeping with town which at first glance a mass of ruins ... "* She found many interesting records there and was touched by the generosity of the people of Pioche. Her next stop was Caliente, and again she wrote, *"No screens and flies are a million thick. Think I have lost my appetite."* The next day Jeanne traveled to Delmar. It was a rough 30-mile ride over many roads that were washed out. She had two oatmeal cookies for lunch and drank water from a cup that tasted like whiskey. Jeanne spent the night in Delmar, where the roof leaked so badly that she had to fold all of her clothes and put them in washstands — even her bed was wet. The next day, on the return trip to Caliente, a wheel fell off of the stagecoach.

Jeanne's diary entry for Saturday, August 1, read, *"Fearfully sultry night. Slept on floor when girl tried to occupy bed with me with her feet in my face ... At supper, heavy thunderstorm came up. Men had to put down tent sides of dining room. Large limb crashed down on roof."*

On Monday, August 3, Jeanne wrote, *"Took pictures of Gentry place and the old Bonnelli house. These oldest in town. Saw a number of old settlements and gained much information. Mr. Syphus is a great tease. Gave me a ten-cent ring for an engagement. Have decided to give up Bunkerville trip. Virgin River too high and heat unendurable. I cannot understand how people live on the Muddy without ice. I would pay $5 to-night for a drink of cold water. My face and body are covered with prickly heat."*

She recorded a trip to Moapa on August 4, and wrote, *"Rose at 3:30 a.m. and took stage for Moapa at 4. So very hot that could scarcely get dressed. Stopped at Logan for breakfast. O. (sic) the filth and dirt of these settlements. Heat too great apparently for people to keep clean. Nevertheless got a good cup of coffee. Reached Moapa at noon. Dinner at Mrs. Powers' and drove to Indian Reservation where purchased five baskets and two water bottles actually in use. Caught train and at 5:30 arrived at Las Vegas where I shall spend a day cleaning up and re-packing. People on the train looked at me as though I had just come out of the wild west show."*

She had a pleasant experience, for a change, August 8 and wrote, *"My room at the Weatley house was paradise when compared with previous accommodations — good carpet, iron bed, large mirror and comfortable rocker. The night too short for today we were to go to El Dorado Canon (sic). We left with one of Mrs. Millier's teams at 10 a.m. and reached the mouth of the canon shortly after 6 p.m. During the last part of the drive the scenery was sublime and the Colorado, when it burst upon our sight, was a stream never to be forgotten. What cordial, gracious people the*

Graceys are. When they heard a woman was coming into camp, a cool white dressing sacque was laid out, a bottle of Pond's Extract for bathing the sunburned face, and everything else that might conduce to the comfort of the traveler — Spent the evening talking of the early days of Nevada."

Jeanne's experience August 10, however, was not as pleasant when she traveled to Nelson to rest. She wrote, "I said we were to 'rest' at Nelson. We did not 'rest,' we 'stayed.' About a dozen men are on a drunk; this was the third day and still there is more to follow. The only lodging in the camp was in a tent just behind the saloon. Until mid-night the air was hideous with oaths, vile language and song. I have never been worse frightened. Fortunately Mr. Williams with me during the early evening and occupied the tent next to mine ... I was glad when we could leave this awful camp and return to Searchlight."

August 11 and 12 found Jeanne at Crescent, where she wrote, "Dressed under difficulties, no water in room, neither a mirror. Toilet has to be made beside front door where passers-by, as well as lodgers passing, could gaze on the operation. Finished breakfast by 6:30 and rode in lumber wagon without springs to Nipton 6 miles distant." On August 13 she wrote, "Could not sleep because of sore arm. Burnt in the sun thro' thin waist. Breakfasted at 6 and left for Jean at 7. Took train for Vegas. Spent day with correspondence and other detail work."

On August 18 she wrote, "Experienced a hard day in Goldfield. People too crazy after gold to care much for history. Mr. Burnett of the Tribune told me in polite language that I was crazy to spend time for the State. But editors of Chronicle-Review and News very cordial and pleasant. Promised to try to secure files."

As Jeanne traveled, she packed and freighted constantly, sending everything of importance back to Reno. On August 22 she visited Mina and wrote, "Mina a young town, about three years old. Two good hotels and a few good houses, many shacks. Telegraphed Reno for money. Traveling in Southern Nevada requires a long purse."

It was almost a month before Jeanne's next entry. She had traveled through the heat of summer into the cooler weather of winter. She was in Rhyolite on October 18 and wrote, *"Wind is blowing furiously and hotel cold. Heated only by stove in lower hall. Had to go to bed to get warm."*

On October 21 she was in Goldfield, staying with the Williams family, where she recorded, *"I wondered last evening where I would sleep for the one room in the cabin does duty for kitchen, dining room and bedroom. At bedtime a large blanket was hung from the rafters before a cot bed, Pullman fashion. It was better than a Pullman too and I slept well in spite of the intense cold. This morning Mr. Williams made a fire and then went out to feed the burro while Mrs. W. and I dressed before the fire. After breakfast, went up to Lee's Camp which is still in process of construction. Shortly before noon, we saddled the horses, and Mr. Williams and I went over the mountains to Old Camp. Made coffee out of snow water at Anderson's cabin. Took pictures, etc. After gathering relics, we tied the packs on the horses and having watered them, started home at 2:30 and arrived there about sundown. Having eaten nothing since breakfast we were ready for a warm meal which Mrs. Williams had in readiness. Never did the fire feel better, for the snow lay over a foot deep in places and a cold wind blew from the east. I am very tired and sore from riding and the bed will feel good."*

As Jeanne completed her pilgrimage for historic relics, she recorded a final entry in her diary October 29 and told of meeting Sam Davis, who related stories of the olden days. He joked that he was afraid to talk to her for fear of being captured for the Museum because nothing was safe when Jeanne Elizabeth Wier was around.

That statement sums up the travels of the intrepid Jeanne Wier. The diary is a testimony of her dedication to the preservation of the past. In Jeanne's tiny date book she recorded more than just moments from history; she recorded a piece of herself. It is the story of an extraordinary woman filled with great strength of character. Jeanne Wier had the gift of seeing the humor in unusual situations and the rare ability to gracefully accept whatever came her way.

Due to the diligent research of Jeanne Wier, the Nevada Historical Society came into being as a private organization in 1904, with several of the state's most prominent men and women as charter members. During the first few years many of the original members became discouraged and dropped out, leaving a small dedicated band determined to prove the society worthy of support. The officers, with secretary and curator Jeanne Wier, never lost sight of their goal. They sought private aid as well as state financing. In 1911, $5,000 was appropriated by the 25th Legislature and approved by the governor for use by the society. Its first building, an unpretentious brick structure, was built near the gates of the University of Nevada. It was rude in appearance, devoid of ornaments, and contained a minimal amount of floor space. Jeanne Wier took more than the usual amount of care to protect the carefully collected contents from fire.

In 1907, the Historical Society was recognized as a state institution and began publishing biennial reports. The society created exhibits and maintained a large correspondence, without clerical assistance. Jeanne Wier continued to work toward her goal of achieving a dignified, safe institution that had space and was conveniently close to the University campus. In 1927 she helped to move the Historical Society to temporary quarters in the State Building in Reno, where it remained until the permanent building it now occupies was completed in 1968.

Today the large modern institution is located on the northeastern portion of the Reno campus of the University of Nevada. It is many times the size of the small unpretentious structure of yesterday, with elaborate exhibits and an active membership. Although Jeanne Wier passed away in 1950, she is still honored as the founder of the Nevada Historical Society. It was her shining light that awakened historic consciousness throughout the state, enabling Nevada to preserve its unique, priceless history and treasures.

If Jeanne Elizabeth Wier were alive today, she would no doubt tell you that her work was not yet complete, for history is endless — there is still the present and the future to be recorded.

The author would like to thank the Nevada Historical Society and Director Peter L. Bandurraga, Ph.D., for the use of their papers and documents of Jeanne Elizabeth Wier.

Jeanne Elizabeth Wier, founder of the Nevada Historical Society

Courtesy of the University of Nevada, Las Vegas

Helen Jane Stewart

Chapter 8

HELEN JANE WISER STEWART

The First Lady of Southern Nevada

Helen Jane Stewart endured loneliness and isolation as she reluctantly followed her husband from one solitary ranch to another. Although it was said she resembled a tiny Dresden China piece, Helen had the strength to shoulder a man's responsibilities while maintaining her gentle femininity. After the brutal murder of her husband, the 30-year-old woman — who was raising five children — successfully took over the management of the Stewarts' 2,000-acre ranch.

Helen Jane Wiser was born April 16, 1854, in Springfield, Illinois. Her parents, Hiram and Delia Wiser, had four other children: three daughters and one son. When Helen was 9 years old, the family moved to the Carson Valley in Nevada, then crossed the Sierra to live in Sacramento, California. She attended public schools in Sacramento and furthered her education at Woodland College in Yuba County, California.

At the age of 18, Helen married Archibald Stewart, a successful Scottish businessman 20 years her senior. Hiram and Delia Wiser had always planned to find older, respectable men to marry their daughters, and Mr. Stewart was quite satisfactory. He was a gentleman of means who operated a freighting business in Nevada. It is not known if the lovely Helen wanted to marry the dour, handsome Scot or if she was even asked.

Following the marriage, Archibald took his youthful bride to live on a ranch at Pony Springs, about 30 miles north of Pioche, Nevada. It was on this lonely ranch that Helen gave birth to her first child, William James. Soon after the baby's arrival, the Stewarts left the isolation of Pony Springs and moved to the town of Pioche, where Helen enjoyed the company of other women. While living at Pioche she had two more children: Hiram Richard, and Flora Eliza Jane, who acquired the nickname of Tiza.

In 1879 Stewart, who had been actively involved in ranching as well as his freighting business, loaned an associate named O. D. Gass $5,000 in gold. Gass offered his 640-acre ranch known as Las Vegas as collateral for the loan, which was to be repaid in 12 months. It was said that the Las Vegas Ranch was an oasis in the middle of a desert valley. The first settlers at the ranch were Mormons sent by Brigham Young in 1855 to establish a mission. One of the men, George Bean, described the property when he wrote, *"We found Las Vegas to be a nice patch of grass about half a mile wide and two or three miles long, situated at the foot of a bench 40 or 50 feet high. The valley faces east, and a pretty clear stream of water, about the size of a common millrace (the current of water that operates a mill wheel), comes from two springs about four miles west of our location. The water of the springs is clear."*[1] The Mormons spent two years at the mission and built several adobe buildings which became the foundation of the original Las Vegas Ranch.

Earlier, in 1868, when Gass had tried to sell the ranch, the state mineralogist wrote a report, saying, *"It had about one hundred and fifty tilled acres. Growing on the ranch were orange, lemon, peach, apple, pear, apricot and fig trees. Pomegranates and grapes were plentiful. Two crops were raised yearly on the same land. The first crop consisted of small grains, such as wheat, barley and oats. These were harvested about the first of June, and then the second crop was planted. This was corn, beans, beets, cabbage, onions, squash, and melons."*[2]

Gass' financial problems did not improve, and in 1880 Stewart received title to the ranch. In 1881 he took control of the land. One year later, when Stewart decided to move his family to Las Vegas, Helen was filled with misgivings. Although the ranch was bountiful, it was in a remote area of a desert wilderness, and brought back memories of her isolation at Pony Springs. Helen was 28 years old and was expecting another child. She begged her husband not to make the move. Thoughts of being completely separated from other women again and of bearing her child alone were terrifying.

1 **History of Las Vegas Mission**, Nevada State Historical Society, papers 1925-1926
2 **Nevada Historical Society Quarterly**, Vol. XVII, No. 1, p. 219.

Because there were no teachers at Las Vegas, Helen also believed the children should have been allowed to remain in Pioche where they were happy and doing well in school. Mr. Stewart, however, was unmoved. He promised they would not remain there long. In April 1882 the family began the long journey across the desert to the out-of-the-way ranch. The "temporary" residence became the Stewarts' home for the rest of their lives.

Helen's fourth child, Evaline La Vega (adopted from her place of birth) Stewart, was born September 22, 1882, without the aid of a midwife or nurse. At that time Mrs. Stewart not only attended to all the chores of the ranch; she had to care for her infant and three young children, who were 3, 6 and 8 years old.

The isolation of the ranch was often broken by guests and travelers who were always welcomed by Helen. She was especially happy to see other women; and although she had Indian help, Helen did all of her own cooking. The visitors usually arrived without advance notice. If they came from the south, she couldn't see them until they were at the door. When they arrived from other directions, Helen could see the dust miles away. Eager for companionship, she would quickly fire up the stove, start potatoes and vegetables cooking, and prepare a pan of biscuits to be put in the oven. The welcomed arrivals were always greeted with the pleasant aroma of fresh coffee.

The ranch prospered; and as money began to accumulate, Helen became worried about being robbed. She was always looking for a safe spot to keep it. While washing windows one day, Helen found a loose board at the top of one window. It concealed a space large enough to hold several sacks. From that day on, Helen kept their money — and that of many prospectors — safely hidden in her secret place.

As with all good things, nothing runs smoothly forever. The tranquility of Las Vegas was shattered in 1884 by the brutal murder of Archibald Stewart. Following a business trip to El Dorado Canyon, Mr. Stewart returned home to find that Schyler Henry, one of his hired hands, had quit. Henry had been spreading scandalous stories about Helen all over the ranch. However, she did not tell her husband about the lies until the morning of the day he was killed.

When Archibald heard what Henry had done, he became so enraged that he went to the Kiel Ranch, where Henry was staying, to avenge his wife's honor. A few hours later Helen received a note from the Kiels. It read, *"Mrs. Stewart send a team and take Mr. Stewart away he is dead. C. Kiel."*

In a letter to her attorney Mrs. Stewart described her husband's murder: *"I left my children with Mr. Fraizer and went as fast as a horse could carry me. The man that killed my husband ran as I approached. As I got to the corner of the house I said oh where is he, oh where is he, and the Old Man Kiel and Hank Parrish said here he is and lifting a blanket showed me the lifeless form of my husband. I knelt down beside him took his hands placed my hand upon his heart and looked upon his face and saw a bullet hole about two inches above the temple."* [1]

Mrs. Stewart also found a bullet hole one inch into his hair. A rifle had been placed directly under his right ear and fired, burning most of the whiskers on that side of his face. He was also shot across the cheekbone and in his shoulder. It was obvious to Helen that her husband had walked into a trap and that there was more than one man involved. As there were no witnesses, the murder was never solved and no one was convicted of the crime. When questioned, Stewart's associates claimed he was a ruthless man in his business deals and had a heartless attitude that created enemies.

Helen and the Indian ranch-hands carefully placed Stewart's remains in the wagon and took him home. When they arrived Helen had the responsibility of burying her husband. As she sadly prepared his body, she realized there was not any planed wood on the ranch with which to build a coffin, so she removed the outside doors of the house to supply the lumber. It was said that Mrs. Stewart skillfully created the box that held her husband's body. The weather was hot, and Archibald Stewart had to be buried the day after his death. He was laid to rest in the hard "caliche" earth in what became known as "The Four Acres," a burial plot that Helen had set aside for the family. Mrs. Stewart was ill as she read the words from the *Episcopal Book of Common Prayer* over the grave of her husband — at that time she was expecting another child.

On July 20, 1884, the *Mohave Miner* printed, *"... No sympathy*

---

1 A letter from Mrs. Stewart to Mr. Sawyer, July 16, 1884, courtesy of Carrie Townley-Porter.

for Stewart was found in El Dorado County, where the general feeling was that he got his just desserts." Following the funeral, Helen was thrust into the management of the ranch. It was business as usual with no time for grief.

Mr. Stewart died without a will and Helen had to appear before the court to gain control of the ranch. She was appointed administratrix of the estate and guardian of her four minor children. The property was divided one-half to the wife and the rest to be shared by the dependents. Although it was customary for a widow to receive a $1,000 tax exemption, the court for reasons unknown refused to grant it in Mrs. Stewart's case. Helen, who was weary from the struggle, accepted the court's decision. Her father temporarily took over Las Vegas, and Mrs. Stewart returned to her parent's home. On January 25, 1885, she gave birth to her fifth and last child, Archibald, who became her favorite.

As soon as Helen was strong enough to travel, she returned to Las Vegas. At first she attempted to sell the large, isolated ranch but had little success. Since she had no choice, Mrs. Stewart took complete control of the property and turned it into the largest holding in Lincoln County, Nevada. Beef was slaughtered, dressed into quarters, and quickly delivered to the miners in El Dorado Canyon. Her days were long, and work was endless. As her sons grew older they helped to run Las Vegas. Hay, grain, vegetables, and fruit were shipped to the market, and the ranch flourished.

With things running smoothly, Helen decided to start a school for the children. Ever since the move to Las Vegas she had been concerned about their lack of education. In 1889 she persuaded a teacher, James Ross Merarrigle, to join her on the ranch. Merarrigle, a graduate of Oxford, had many talents. He could sing, play a fiddle, write poetry, and converse freely on most subjects. An intellectual bond between the small, lonely woman and the aging man was quickly established. They shared literary subjects and enjoyed each other's company. Merarrigle took care of the legal documents in addition to teaching the children. He was happy at Las Vegas and filled a gap in Helen's life for five years until his death in 1894. Mrs. Stewart took care of the services of her dear friend, and there were two graves in "The Four Acres."

In March of 1886, Frank Roger Stewart — no relation to Archibald — had been hired as a ranch-hand at Las Vegas. Frank was a wanderer who was accomplished at many things. After Merarrigle's death, Helen was lonely and she began to rely on Stewart for help and advice. He assisted with the ledgers, helped nurse her children through illnesses, and even lent a hand making preserves. It appeared that Frank Stewart had found a home at the ranch.

As isolated as the ranch was, there were parties and guests. Las Vegas was the cultural and social center of Lincoln County. In 1893 it became the site of the post office. Helen was appointed post-mistress, and it was called Los Vegas Post Office to prevent confusion with one in Las Vegas, New Mexico.

As Hiram and William matured, Helen sent the girls and her young son Archie to Los Angeles to further their schooling. Although Helen hated to part with her beloved Archie, she realized the importance of an education. She wrote him constantly and worried when there was no reply. On his 14th birthday Helen wrote him this letter:

"This is your birthday. You are 14 years old. I wonder what course you will pursue. What will you do? What kind of man will you be? I think you have pride and manliness about you to try and be one of the best. Remember always that I love you and always think of you every day and wonder what you are doing."

Helen didn't have to wonder about Archie's future for long because it would be his last birthday. In July the boy was chasing wild horses on the ranch and fell from his horse. Mrs. Stewart, who was visiting Los Angeles, sadly returned to bury her favorite child in "The Four Acres" next to the father he had never known.

Archie's death was almost more than Helen could bear. She was weary and wanted to sell Las Vegas. The other children deeded their shares to her, giving their mother complete control over the ranch. In 1902 Mrs. Stewart sold Las Vegas to the railroad. She kept "The Four Acres" plus 160 acres and water rights. By 1903, 21 years after she had arrived at the ranch, Helen was finally free. Tragedy, however, struck the same year when her older son Hiram developed pneumonia and died after a brief illness. Following his funeral, Helen placed another grave in "The Four Acres."

The sale of her ranch left her with time on her hands, and the loss of Hiram was painful. Although she could have married earlier, Mrs. Stewart had preferred to remain a widow. But later in 1903, the 49-year-old woman married her former ranch-hand, Frank Stewart. He signed a premarital agreement just before the ceremony, as Helen did not intend to lose control over her estate or her independence. Throughout her marriage to Frank, Helen was the dominant partner. Frank never enjoyed the full status of a husband; he became her companion.

The Frank Stewarts moved into a new house on Helen's property at Las Vegas, across the street from the old ranch. Civilization had finally caught up with what had once been a lonely spot in the desert. Helen had been away from culture so long that she almost forgot the social amenities. With the arrival of many prominent ladies, Mrs. Stewart was suddenly thrown back into the stream of fashionable affairs. Carrie Townley-Porter shared some humorous incidents in her story, *Helen Jane Stewart, The First Lady of Las Vegas*, published in *The Nevada Historical Society Quarterly*. She wrote:

The arrival of Mary Bates Park, bride of William S. Park, created a state of excitement, even among women who had been living in areas not so isolated as the Vegas Ranch. Mrs. Park, accustomed to the strict rules of etiquette accepted by the plantation society of Kentucky, did not understand the anxiety created among the women living in Las Vegas. She wasted no time in entertaining the Las Vegas ladies in her new home at Fourth and Fremont. The women invited to the gala affair were thrown into a dither because many did not own a hat, and they simply could not make an appearance without one. A plan was soon devised whereby a group of women attended wearing the available hats, then, after leaving the Park home, each quickly turned her hat over to a friend, enabling all to attend the affair ... Mrs. Park indicated puzzlement at the duplication of several chapeaus adorning the women. To add to her confusion, Helen Stewart entered the house, went through the receiving line, and immediately esconced (sic) herself in a rocking chair in the dining room. There she proceeded to rock for the remainder of the afternoon. Mrs. Park was aghast at such behavior. The rigid rules to which she was accustomed stipulated almost to the exact minute how long a guest stayed at such functions. She appealed to Delphine Squires for assistance. Mrs. Squires helped Mrs. Park understand the situation in which Helen Stewart had lived for twenty years, when every guest in her home was welcome to stay in terms of days, not minutes.

Mrs. Stewart quickly became a part of the social activities. She was popular for her gentle, unassuming manner and genuine interest in others. Helen was always interested in history and her new home was filled with exquisite Indian baskets and valuable artifacts. She became the first president of the Las Vegas Historical Society and a close friend of historian Jeanne Elizabeth Wier. Mrs. Stewart was delighted to participate in women's clubs. She was elected to the Clark County School Board and was among the first women in the county to serve on a jury.

On April 10, 1914, her son Will's second wife, Mina, gave birth to a daughter who they named Helen Jane Stewart. The family did not realize for several months, however, that a difficult delivery had left the little girl mentally retarded. Helen developed a deep love for her namesake and exceptional granddaughter. She took pleasure in each of the child's small steps forward. Because of this special little girl and Helen's help, the Helen J. Stewart School for Retarded Children was founded in Las Vegas.

In 1918 the family discovered that Helen's husband Frank was suffering from terminal cancer of the throat. As Helen nursed him through a long, painful illness, she began to lose her own strength. When Mr. Stewart died she was physically worn out. Although Helen had loved her second husband, he was not buried in "The Four Acres." Even in death Frank Stewart remained outside the family.

Mrs. Stewart slowly regained her health and enjoyed a quiet life until 1924, when she was diagnosed as having cancer. Unfortunately it was inoperable at her age. Helen calmly accepted the fact and turned over all her personal property and home to her remaining children. Helen, who had spent a lifetime caring for others, became dependent upon those she loved and those who loved her. During her last months Helen Stewart was not forgotten by her many friends and family members. Flowers filled her home and visitors constantly dropped by to see her. Although she was in constant pain, Mrs. Stewart retained her charm and wit as well as an interest in the activities around her. On March 6, 1926, at the age of 72, Helen Jane Stewart passed away.

Her funeral procession was the largest ever witnessed in Las Vegas, and the local businesses closed for the day in respect of their most honored pioneer. The words of one of Helen's close friends, Delphine Squires, provided a suitable epitaph for this remarkable woman. It reads, *"Her frail little body housed an indomitable will, a wonderful strength of purpose, and a courageous heart, and she faced death as she had faced the everyday problems of life, with sublime fortitude."*

The author would like to thank the Nevada Historical Society and Director Peter L. Bandurraga, Ph.D., for the use of the Nevada Historical Society Quarterly, *Vol. XVII, No. 1, Spring, 1974, and Carrie Townley-Porter for her delightful story,* Helen J. Stewart, The First Lady of Las Vegas, *and the use of her notes and articles. Mrs. Townley-Porter has a forthcoming book about the life of Helen Jane Stewart.*

Mr. Sawyer, Sir,

I write to you in great distress of mind. Hoping you as a husband and a father will aid me to the best of your ability. I am left all alone and my little children fatherless by the hand of a murderer. My beloved husband was murdered Sunday at Mr. Kiels ranch one mile and a half from here while defending the honor of his family from a black-hearted slanderous tongue. The evidence is all circumstantial. The man had been working here a while, and while Mr. Stewart was in El Dorado Canyon, left and went over to the Kiels and was kept posted on every movement going on at the Vegas and was supplied with arms and a house by men on the Ranch ... Archie came home Sunday about 10 o'clock. After he had eaten and rested a short time I told him of the slander being talked about to everyone stopping by our place and passers by the day before Mr. Stewart came home. They tried to frighten me with paying the man Schyler Henry off and letting him go. As he got money and clothing of Mr. Stewart which knew nothing of I could not settle as it was something I had never done before. About two o'clock Willie the oldest boy said his father saddled his horse ... going off in the opposite direction than the Kiels. I supposed he was going down to George Allen at his camp ... The next I heard of my poor husband was the note which I copied as it was written by old man Kiel ... It was evident Mr. Stewart was in the house with no one as witness except this Henry and old man Kiel. They are both Archie's enemies and would not tell the truth but swear against Archie. I am here with a lot of roughs and my life and husband's property in danger ... The man that murdered my husband is still at Kiels with a slight flesh wound in the hip. It is dangerous to say or do anything as we are overpowered by numbers and in distress.

Yours in Distress,
Mrs. Archie Stewart

◆ ──────────────────────────────── ◆

Helen Jane Stewart as a young girl

Archibald Stewart

Helen Stewart at the time of her marriage to Archibald

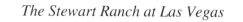

The Stewart Ranch at Las Vegas

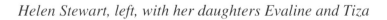

Helen Stewart, left, with her daughters Evaline and Tiza

Courtesy of the Grace Hudson Museum

Grace Carpenter Hudson

Chapter 9

GRACE CARPENTER HUDSON
✦ ✦
A Lady With a Paint Brush

A lthough her painting was considered daring because of the subject matter, Grace Carpenter Hudson became one of the most accomplished Western artists in America. During the late 1800s there was an almost insatiable demand for the work of this talented lady who captured the beauty of a unique people on canvas. While Grace brought attention to the heartwarming shyness of the Pomo Indians, her husband John recorded their customs and language. Together they preserved the heritage of a culture for posterity.

"On February 21, 1865, the Ukiah Herald (a local California newspaper) announced the arrival of not one, but two, young Carpenters. The boy was named Grant, the girl Grace."[1] The Carpenters, a pioneer family that participated in the Western migration, arrived safely from Kansas in 1859 and became respected citizens in the Potter Valley area near Ukiah.

Grace's father, Aurelius O. "Reel" Carpenter, was a newspaper man and professional photographer. Her mother, Helen McCowen, was an educated woman from a family of strong-willed women. Grace's grandmother, Clarina Howard Nichols, a fiery speaker, once advised women to refuse to marry unless they were given the vote.

The twins' childhood was spent on a pleasant farm where the family raised most of its own food. Because the Indian children were among Grace's first playmates, she learned the ways of the Pomo as a small child. The Indians were in awe of Grant and Grace. The birth of twins in the Pomo culture was rare and usually ended with the Indians putting both infants to death. They believed that twinning was caused by evil and if the children lived they would

1 **The Painter Lady, Grace Carpenter Hudson,** Searles R. Boynton, D.D.S., Sun House Guild Corporation, Ukiah, CA, 1978.

eventually harm each other. However, because Grant and Grace were white, they were accepted and looked upon with great curiosity.

While Helen and her daughter May nursed the twins through their first years, Reel Carpenter had two jobs. He divided his time between the ranch and photography. In 1869 the family left Potter Valley for Ukiah so Reel could expand his photography business. The move was a good one for Reel, whose photographic skills were appreciated in Ukiah where he became known as "the picture man."

In 1878, 13-year-old Grace left her home to attend Normal School in San Francisco. She spent two years at the school and began to study art at the California School of Design. Within a short time it was obvious that the young woman had a rare talent. Her ability developed fast, and she was soon filling her canvases with anatomical drawings and landscapes. She also assisted her father by hand-coloring portraits of his clientele. At the age of 16, Grace Carpenter received the Alvord Gold Medal for the best full-length study in crayon. This was quite an achievement for an art pupil who had studied only 18 months.

By the time Grace was 18, she had matured into an attractive young woman with several admirers. The gentleman she chose to wed, however, was William T. Davis, a man of 33 who did not receive the Carpenters' approval. Reel thought William was culturally beneath his daughter, and Helen was quite outspoken, refusing to let Davis visit their home. Grace, who possessed the high-spirited ways of her mother and grandmother, calmly continued her relationship with Davis. In 1884, when Grace was 19, the couple were wed, only to receive a divorce 15 months later. The unhappy months of her marriage showed in Grace's work, and she returned home to Ukiah. Since a divorce in the 1800s was considered a disgrace, it was almost two years before Grace was invited to attend social events and parties. During that time she became an unassuming, modest woman, and at the age of 22 Grace was ready to resume her promising career.

In 1889 Ukiah became the home of John Wilz Napier Hudson, M.D., from Nashville, Tennessee. Hudson was a handsome young man who became the most sought-after bachelor in town. All the eligible ladies of Ukiah were anxious to meet the charming doctor, and they could hardly wait for the first social event. The opportunity arrived in April at the first annual ball of the Native Sons of the Golden West. Among the elegantly dressed ladies attending the dance was Mrs. Grace Davis, who completely stole the heart of the distinguished doctor.

Dr. Hudson quickly became a respected member of the community, and later that year Grace opened her art studio to the public. The handsome young couple were seen everywhere together. The tall, dark physician and the lovely, petite Grace made a striking pair. Thirteen months after John's arrival, they were married. Following the wedding they temporarily lived with the Carpenters, then moved into Grace's studio.

The marriage to John changed Grace's professional life. Her previous work had been done for experience, without direction. Portraying the Pomo Indian became her new goal. She found art in the Indians; and since she knew her subjects well, Grace Hudson painted them with feeling and detail.

Her first painting depicted the child of a woman who came to do the Hudsons' washing. The infant, who was tied into a little wicker cradle, was propped in a corner while the mother did her work. Mrs. Hudson suggested the baby be brought inside for warmth, then she made stolen trips to the corner to do preliminary sketches as the child slept. It was difficult to paint the Indians, for they were superstitious. Most believed that the native who allowed a person to make a likeness of him gave that person the power of life over him. Others believed that to be painted or "captured" meant death.

Before Grace completed her painting of the child, a buyer from the East visited her studio and became interested in her picture. He was struck by the subject as well as the treatment Grace gave it. When he returned a few weeks later to purchase the painting, Grace was amazed at the amount of money he paid and his offer to buy more. This served to increase the artist's desire to paint the Pomo Indians. Her work soon became so popular that each picture sold immediately. Many were reproduced in newspapers, and her "Turnip

Baby" was the leading illustration for a magazine article on children.

John Hudson, an independent man who did not fit into a structured career, was also drawn to the Native Americans. Although Hudson was a physician, he chose to spend the rest of his life studying and documenting the anthropology and ethnology of the Indians. He began collecting artifacts and learning their customs and language. Eventually Hudson found himself so absorbed in this new field that he gave up his medical practice. While John recorded the Pomo Indian culture, Grace brought the people to life on canvas. The doctor's interest and encouragement in Grace's work helped to lead her to greater success.

With the sale of her first painting, Grace began numbering each canvas. To further preserve her collection, she kept a notebook listing descriptions, dimensions, dates of completion, and the new owners. Grace not only painted the Pomo; she wrote a historical background and story to accompany each picture.

During the 1800s, Indians were usually considered by the white man to be aborigines belonging to an inferior race. Many people could not accept the fact that such a lovely, talented woman painted Indians. In the book *The Painter Lady*, author Searles R. Boynton, D.D.S., described the following scene and conversation.

"As usual, Grace Hudson's skill with brush and oil was sufficient to arouse comment. When the paintings of Mollie and Powley were placed on exhibit in an art room in San Francisco, three onlookers were overheard to relate the following series of comments: 'Well, she paints Indians!' said the first. The companion next to him replied, excitedly, 'She paints Indians!' Whereupon the third and final play upon emphasis was made as the last gentleman declared, with conviction, 'She paints Indians! ...'"[1]

When asked how she got her babies to pose, Mrs. Hudson once said, *"They are regular little stoics. They will sit and stare at you without blinking an eye or moving a muscle while I perform the most grotesque antics in order to provoke a laugh ... I worked three days on a baby before I could get a smile, and then only by putting on a feather headdress and dancing around like an Apache medi-*

---

1 **The Painter Lady, Grace Carpenter Hudson,** Searles R. Boynton, D.D.S., Sun House Guild Corporation, Ukiah, CA, 1978. A quote from a newspaper article of that period.

cine man. I worried, tormented, bullied and frightened one poor little fellow for two days trying to make him cry. I grew ashamed of myself and gave it up. But when I tried to pacify him with candy and beads he yelled lustily, and I got a splendid photograph of him." [1]

Grace was a loving human being who showed it in her sense of humor and natural charm. She also enjoyed fancy clothing and was always seen in public wearing the latest fashions. Many of her dresses were hand-painted with floral designs on the bodice and underskirt. She liked elbow-length sleeves with inner ruffles of white organdy. Her scarves were of silk; her handkerchiefs embroidered with dates; and her hats trimmed with feathers and flowers. Yet, when she was at work, Mrs. Hudson could be seen wearing a large, plain apron. When Grace hunted, she wore the appropriate apparel to climb the hills with her dog and gun. Grace was an ardent sportswoman, a crack-shot, and an expert swimmer.

In 1893 Mrs. Hudson painted "Little Mendocino," a painting that became her first major canvas and a popular attraction at well-known exhibits and art shows. As Grace became increasingly admired, the public wanted to know more about the artist and what she looked like. The *Illustrated Pacific States* published this article in September 1894:

We give in this number a portrait of the widely-known artist, Mrs. Grace Carpenter Hudson, which surely cannot fail to please. The handsome face which smiles back at us from the page would be most attractive, even if the interest arising from her fame as an artist should not lend its added charm.

There is an indication of her genius in the bright, magnetic expression, which all will notice, and besides, there is such a suggestion of sweetness and pleasantry in her face that none can discredit the lovable character they evidence.

Mrs. Hudson enjoys a wide and well-deserved reputation for her pictures of Indians. She has shown remarkable skill in depicting the dark-skinned children of the wigwam and the forest, and gives us glimpses of wild babyhood, as rare as they are touching. In her unique specialty, she stands without rival. Her pictures are lifelike, and her work is the more worthy of commendation in consideration of the difficulties to be sur-

The New York Evening Sun, Thursday, November 7, 1895

mounted in painting from such peculiar and busy, unpathetic (sic) models.

Born amid rural scenes in Mendocino County, of parents who are as honest and truthful as God's harmonious nature surrounding her birthplace, Mrs. Hudson enjoys a combination of advantages rarely enjoyed by any other natural-born artist.

Mr. Morris, of Morris and Kennedy, who is acknowledged to be an excellent critic, says of her work, "We have had for sale and on exhibition a number of Mrs. Hudson's pictures, and they universally received the highest admiration and praise. Some of her larger canvases bring as high as $500, and smaller ones from $150 up. Such prices give ample testimony of her skill and popularity. I know of no California artist who gives promise of greater success than lies in her power to achieve; and I believe, with time and a wider field, her talent will acquire national fame."

Personally, Mrs. Hudson is as bright and charming as her portrait suggests. Of the brunette type, slight and graceful, she is gifted with uncommon attractions; but, besides, one finds in her that power of intellect and brilliance of perception which in themselves seem winning charms enough.[1]

In 1902 Grace Hudson felt weary. She had been painting without rest for over 10 years and began to feel the need to change her subjects. The Hudsons had no children of their own, and Mr. Hudson was gone most of the time. He had advanced far in his chosen field and gathered a collection of artifacts that was receiving worldwide acclaim. The Field Museum of Chicago had appointed John to the position of collector of the institution, which further separated him from his wife. Grace needed new, unfamiliar horizons, so she set sail for the Hawaiian Islands.

Her letters to John during that time revealed a tiredness that was unusual for her and the fact that she deeply loved and missed him. John, too, was lonely. He wanted her to give up painting as a career and pursue it for pleasure only. Grace, however, was soon painting in earnest again, this time using Hawaiians for models. Almost a year later when she left the Islands, Grace had completed 27 paintings.

1 **The Painter Lady, Grace Carpenter Hudson,** Searles R. Boynton, D.D.S., Sun House Guild Corporation, Ukiah, CA 1978.

When she returned to Ukiah, John joined her. The separation had strengthened their love. They took an extended tour of Europe; and in 1906, when the Hudsons visited San Francisco, they found the catastrophic earthquake had destroyed many of Grace's valuable canvases. In 1910 the couple decided to build a house in Ukiah where they could work together. Grace was 45 years old, and she needed security and the company of her husband.

Their new home, The Sun House, was completed in 1912. The carefully-crafted, two-story structure designed by Grace and John was built with an eye toward the artist. Its spacious rooms and many windows provided a perfect background for Grace, allowing her to move in freedom with her easel, without the loss of light. The Sun House is now California Historical Landmark No. 926 and is listed in the National Register of Historic Places.

In 1920, when she was 55, Grace suffered from a thyroid condition. Although doctors recommended surgery, the Hudsons decided to have radium tubes implanted in the artist's neck. Since she was a vain lady, Grace wore high necklines for the rest of her life to hide the ugly red marks caused by the implants. She continued to turn out perfect paintings.

As Grace neared her 70th birthday, John Hudson became ill and needed constant care. He died January 20, 1936, and Grace Hudson never painted again. On March 23, 1937, Mrs. Hudson followed her husband in death. Without John, Grace had little to live for.

During her lifetime, the talented lady created at least 684 paintings. She was one of the most dedicated artists of her era, who overcame insurmountable obstacles when she chose the Pomo Indians as her subject. Although her pictures have been exhibited in the leading cities of Europe and the United States, her most valued contribution was in preserving and lending dignity to an exceptional people.

The story of Grace Carpenter Hudson has been made possible through the generosity of The Grace Hudson Museum and Sun House, and from the book The Painter Lady, Grace Carpenter Hudson *by Searles R. Boynton, D.D.S., Sun House Guild Corporation, Ukiah, California, 1978.*

Courtesy of the Grace Hudson Museum, Acc #18339

◆───────────────────────◆

John Wilz Napier Hudson

Courtesy of the Grace Hudson Museum, Acc #18391

◆―――――――――――――――――――――――◆

Grace Hudson, Ukiah's noted artist

◆ ━━━━━━━━━━━━━━━━━━━━━━━━━━ ◆

Carpenter family portrait, circa 1873

Grace is to the right of her father.

Courtesy of the Grace Hudson Museum, Acc #541

◆———————————————————◆

Grace Hudson's painting of "The Bride"

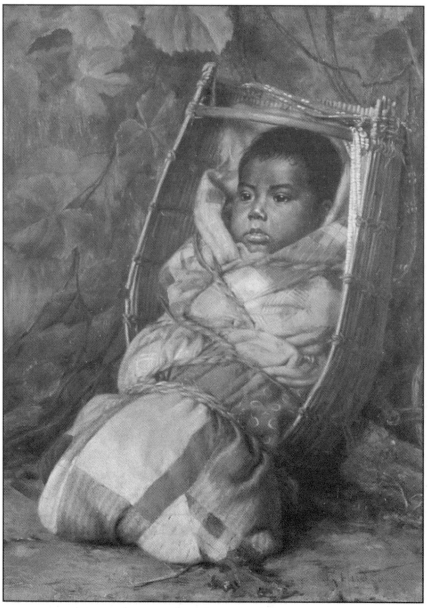

"Mr. Dr. Hudson Billy-Bow-Legs," by Grace Hudson

◆ ━━━━━━━━━━━━━━━━━━━━━ ◆

Grace Hudson with her pet kittens

BIBLIOGRAPHY

Primary Sources:

Chapter 1. Jessie Benton Frémont
Newspapers: *San Francisco Chronicle*, Dec. 28, 1902; *Oakland Tribune*, Aug. 3, 1969. Books: *A Man Unafraid,* by Herbert Bashford and Harr Wagner, 1928; *Jessie Benton Frémont*, by Pamela Herr, 1987. *Jessie Benton Frémont*, Sally Roesch Wagner's lecture.

Chapter 2. Abigail Scott Duniway
Excerpts from *Eliza Lafayette Bristow's letters* and *Pioneer Women of Oregon,* by Olga Freeman, courtesy of the Oregon Historical Society, Portland, Oregon. Books: *Rebel For Rights*, by Ruth Barnes Moynihan, 1985; *Pathbreaking*, by Abigail Scott Duniway, 1971.

Chapter 3. Sarah Winnemucca
Newspapers and Periodicals: *The Californian*, September 1882; *Reese Reveille*, Feb. 12, 1885; *Nevada State Journal*, Feb. 12, 1872; *Sarah Winnemucca's Practical Solution to the Indian Problem*, by Elizabeth Peabody. Books: *Life Among the Paiutes*, by Sarah Winnemucca, 1886; *Sarah Winnemucca of the Northern Paiutes*, by Gae Whitney, 1931.

Chapter 4. Fanny Stenhouse and Ann Eliza Young
Books: *The Tyranny of Mormonism*, by Fanny Stenhouse, 1888; *Isn't One Wife Enough*, by Kimball Young, 1958; *Handcarts to Zion*, by LeRoy and Ann Halfen, 1960.

Chapter 5. Belle Starr
Notes, letters, newspaper articles and documents from *The Edna Gaither Collection, William Tilghman Collection, Charles B. Rhodes Collection*, courtesy of the Western History Collections, University of Oklahoma, Norman, Oklahoma.

BIBLIOGRAPHY

Books: *Belle Starr, The Bandit Queen*, by Burton Roscoe, 1941; *Belle Starr and Her Times*, by Glenn Shirley, 1982.

Chapter 6. Nellie Cashman

Newspapers: *Frontier Angel, The West*, July 1972; *Tucson Star*, Jan. 7 1992; *Tombstone Epitaph*, Nov. 3, 1881; *Tucson Citizen*, Dec. 7, 1929, April 5, 1965, and April 19, 1971; *Daily Colonist*, Victoria, B.C., March 1898 and Jan. 1, 1925; *British Colonist*, Victoria, B.C.,June 1876-1905; *Arizona Star*, Jan. 8, 1924; *Bisbee Daily Review*, April 1, 1948 and Feb. 1, 1959; *Arizona Highway*, February 1987.

Books: *Nellie Cashman*, by John P. Clum, 1931.

Chapter 7. Jeanne Elizabeth Wier

The Diary of Jeanne Wier, Nevada Historical Quarterly, Vol. 17, No. 3, 1974; *Nevada Historical Society Papers*, 1913-1916.

Chapter 8. Helen Jane Stewart

Notes, letters, newspaper articles and documents, Carrie Townley-Porter, Reno; *Helen Jane Stewart, The First Lady of Las Vegas*, Carrie Townley-Porter, from the *Nevada Historical Society Quarterly*, Vol. XVII, No. 1.

Chapter 9. Grace Carpenter Hudson

Newspapers: *The New York Evening Sun*, Nov. 7, 1895.

Books: *The Painter Lady, Grace Carpenter Hudson*, by Searles R. Boynton, D.D.S., 1979, courtesy of the Sun House Guild; *History of Mendocino and Lake County*, by Aurelius O. Carpenter and Percy H. Millbury 1914.

BOOKS

Bashford, Herbert and Wagner, Herr, *A Man Unafraid*, 1928

Benton, Beverly, *The Women's Suffrage Movement 1869-1968*, 1986

Boynton, Searles R., D.D.S., *The Painter Lady, Grace Carpenter Hudson*, 1979

Breehan, Carl, *The Bandit Belle*, 1970

Brown, Dee, *Gentle Tamers*, 1974

Clappe, Shirley, *The Shirley Letters*, 1970

Clum, John P., *Nellie Cashman*, 1931

Duniway, Abigail Scott, *Pathbreaking*, 1971

Gray, Dorothy, *Women of the West*, 1979

Halfen, LeRoy and Ann, *Handcarts to Zion*, 1960

Herr, Pamela, *Jessie Benton Fremont*, 1987

Hicks, Edwin, *Belle Starr and Her Pearl*, 1963

Horan, James D., *Desperate Women*, 1944

Luchetti, Cathy, *Women of the West*, 1982

Mayer, Melanie, *Klondike Women*, 1989

Morrison, Dorothy Nafus, *Chief Sarah*, 1980

Morrison, Dorothy Nafus, *Ladies Were Not Expected*, 1985

Morrison, Dorothy Nafus, *Under A Strong Wind*, 1983

Moynihan, Ruth Barnes, *Rebel For Rights*, 1985

Reiter, Joan Swallow, *The Women*, 1978

Richey, Elinor, *Eminent Women of the West*, 1975

Roscoe, Burton, *Belle Starr, The Bandit Queen*, 1941

Ross, Nancy, *Westward the Women*, 1944

Shirley, Glenn, *Belle Starr and Her Times*, 1982

Sifakis, Carl, *The Encyclopedia of American Crime*, 1892

Sinclair, Andrew, *The Better Half*, 1965

Stenhouse, Fanny, *The Tyranny of Mormonism*, 1888

Wallace, Irving, *The Twenty-Seventh Wife*, 1961

Whitney, Gae, *Sarah Winnemucca of the Northern Paiutes*, 1931

Williams, Paul, *A Dynasty of Western Outlaws*, 1961

Young, Kimball, *Isn't One Wife Enough*, 1958

Order these exciting books, by
Western author Anne Seagraves, Today!

Thank you for your order!